M**O**THER
I Am a

M*I Am a*OTHER

JANE CLAYSON JOHNSON

WITH A FOREWORD BY SHERI DEW

DESERET
BOOK

SALT LAKE CITY, UTAH

Library of Congress Cataloging-in-Publication Data

Johnson, Jane Clayson.
  I am a mother / Jane Clayson Johnson ; foreword by Sheri Dew.
      p. cm.
  Includes bibliographical references and index.
  ISBN-13: 978-1-59038-717-7 (hardback : alk. paper)
  ISBN-10: 1-59038-717-1 (hardback : alk. paper)
    1. Motherhood—Religious aspects—Mormon Church. 2. Mothers—Religious life. 3. Church of Jesus Christ of Latter-day Saints—Doctrines. 4. Mormon Church—Doctrines. I. Title.
  BX8641.J633 2007
  248.8'4310882893—dc22   2006036441

Printed in the United States of America
Publishers Printing, Salt Lake City, UT

10   9   8   7   6   5   4   3   2   1

For my mother

CONTENTS

FOREWORD BY SHERI DEW ix

ACKNOWLEDGMENTS xiii

INTRODUCTION xv

CHAPTER ONE: I AM A MOTHER 1

CHAPTER TWO: A PENCIL IN THE HAND OF GOD—MY STORY 18

CHAPTER THREE: WHY IT MATTERS 40

CHAPTER FOUR: A MOTHER'S INFLUENCE 53

CHAPTER FIVE: CAN I QUIT NOW? 71

CHAPTER SIX: WALKING IN EACH OTHER'S SHOES 96

CHAPTER SEVEN: WE ARE ALL MOTHERS 112

WORKS CITED 129

INDEX 133

FOREWORD

It may be precisely because I have not had the privilege of bearing children that I feel so deeply about the majesty and magnificence of motherhood. For in some instances, absence makes the heart grow fonder. And that is certainly the case with me. My longing and pleading for the blessing of motherhood has stretched beyond several decades now, and because of that, perhaps I've paid unusual attention to the impact and influence of mothers.

More than sixty years ago, the First Presidency said it all when they called motherhood "the highest, holiest service . . . assumed by mankind" (*Improvement Era*, November 1942, 761). Simply stated, everything I have experienced and everything

I have observed tells me this doctrine, the doctrine of mother-hood, is true.

Have you ever wondered why prophets have taught this doctrine again and again and again? I have. I've thought long and hard about the work of women of God. And I've wrestled with what the doctrine of motherhood means for all of us. This issue has driven me to my knees, to the scriptures, and to the temple! In each of those places I have found reinforcement of this ennobling doctrine. It is a doctrine each of us must understand if we hope to be steadfast and immovable in the face of the complex and confusing issues that swirl around our gender. For Satan has declared war on motherhood. He knows that those who rock the cradle have the power to rock his earthly empire. And he knows that without righteous mothers loving and leading the next generation, the kingdom of God will fail.

Through her mothering, a woman is the consummate leader of leaders. If we truly believe that we are here in mortality to be tested and to demonstrate by the way we live our lives whether we want to be part of the kingdom of God or not, then what could possibly be more significant than bearing a child and thus making it possible for a spirit son or daughter to advance beyond the preparatory state of premortal life and enter the testing stage of earth life? And having borne that child, what could possibly be more enduring or important in the eyes of our Heavenly

Father than nurturing one of His sons or daughters—teaching and cheering that precious soul on, preparing him or her to pass the test?

Nothing. No diplomat or CEO or billionaire philanthropist does anything that comes anywhere close in importance to what a mother does. No trophy or status or honor of man begins to compare with motherhood in terms of its eternal impact and glory. Period.

Now, the world won't tell you that because the adversary knows full well the power of a righteous, determined mother. That is why this is an important book, one well worth reading.

By the world's standard, Jane Clayson Johnson had it made. She's bright, she's gorgeous, and at one point in her life was appearing daily before millions. But she gave it all up—at least, that's how the world would view it—to become a mother. She is the first to say that motherhood isn't always easy and doesn't always feel supernally rewarding, but she is also the first to declare that what she is now doing to nurture the little ones who've been entrusted to her far outweighs in impact and importance anything she did before.

If the day comes when we—meaning covenant women of God—are the only women on earth who find nobility and divinity in motherhood, so be it. For *mother* is the word that will define a righteous woman made perfect in the highest degree of the celestial kingdom, a woman who has qualified for eternal increase in posterity, wisdom, joy, and influence.

Jane Johnson is a living example of someone who believes and is acting on that principle.

Sheri Dew

ACKNOWLEDGMENTS

I am indebted to many people who have each in some way contributed to this book.

Thank you to my friend Whitney Johnson. From first outline to final edits, she was there—hosting focus groups, transcribing interviews, suggesting scriptures and quotes. And during those many moments when I felt completely discouraged or overwhelmed, she was the angel in my ear telling me over and over, "Yes, you can. You can do this . . ."

A very special thank you also to Janna DeVore. She was an extraordinary gift to me during this process and innately shares the spirit and the message of this book.

Profound thanks to Jana Erickson, who was an important champion of this project within Deseret Book; Richard Peterson, for his sensitive and astute editing; Sheryl Smith, for her beautiful cover design; Laurie Cook, for her typesetting skills; and of course, Sheri Dew, under whose leadership Deseret Book has greatly expanded its sphere of influence and ability to touch and uplift lives, and whose own voice has become a beacon throughout the world.

Thank you to all the women who told me their stories . . . and trusted me to share them. Thank you to my friends near and far who gave me their wonderful insights on the many versions of this manuscript.

Thank you to my dad, who calls me nearly every day just to tell me he loves me and to encourage me no matter what I'm doing. To my mom, whose example has shaped me in every way as a woman and as a mother. To my sister, Hannah, who is younger than I, but has always been my example and my light.

To my husband, Mark, who is honorable to the core and whose depth of faith inspires me every day.

And finally, to my children, I love you. And I am so grateful to be able to say, I am your mother.

INTRODUCTION

Your success as a family . . . our success as a nation . . .
depends not on what happens inside the White House,
but on what happens inside your house.

—Barbara Bush, *Barbara Bush: A Memoir,* 570

Nearly ten years ago I listened to Elder Jeffrey R. Holland give what has since become one of my favorite talks. In it, he said this: "Mothers go longer on less sleep and give more to others with less personal renewal for themselves than any other group I know at any other time in life. It is not surprising when the shadows under their eyes sometimes vaguely resemble the state of Rhode Island" ("Because She Is a Mother," 36–37).

At the time I didn't have any children, so I thought that statement was a slight exaggeration. After all, nothing could really be *that* tiring, could it? Well, after having two babies in the last two years, I can say with complete conviction that the bags under my eyes more closely match the dimensions of Texas—not Rhode Island.

Other than that, Elder Holland was right on!

No question about it, mothering is a tough job. Pulitzer-prize-winning author and mother Anna Quindlen so eloquently refers to motherhood as "the work of the ages," tantamount to building a great nation.

"If any of us engaged in the work of mothering thought much about it as the task of fashioning the fine points of civilization," she writes, "we would be frozen into immobility by the enormity of the task" (*Loud and Clear*, 57).

Frozen is right! Some days I look around and feel so overwhelmed by the day ahead of me I don't know where to start. And other times, when I least expect it, I am stopped in my tracks by society's slights to motherhood or by a slew of expert advice on how to become Supermom.

It is, in part, experiencing those moments that has led to this book. Because, at other times, when quiet is allowed to seep into my heart and leads me to prayer and reflection, I have learned for myself that mothers matter. I matter. And so do you.

It is that message I hope to share in this book. For all too often I think mothers—women in general, really—tend to forget their great worth. We become discouraged or guilt-ridden or just plain exhausted and don't realize that what we do every day has enormous impact and implication. We get caught up in judging one another or taking sides and forget that the work of mothers is God's work—and because it is his work, he will help us and lift us up and make us stronger.

The seeds of this book began to grow during my son William's 4:00 A.M. feedings. As I would rock that little baby in my arms and think about my calling as a mother juxtaposed with my years in television, my mind would be flooded with ideas—a line or a paragraph or a story would come to me about motherhood and its significance.

In the wee hours of many mornings, my husband would come downstairs to check on me . . . and smile . . . as I sat at the kitchen table scribbling on a notepad or tapping on the computer.

From the depths of my heart, I believe that the experiences of my life have brought me to this moment to be able to proclaim this message: Motherhood matters. I want every woman to believe this, to feel it in her soul, and embrace it.

As you read, I hope you will feel the power that exists within women and mothers. I also hope you will remember one other thing: My path is not your path, and your path is unique to you. We must all make choices based on our own circumstances and desires. Just like our children—who have the uncanny ability to be completely different from one another despite their similar genetic makeup—we are all distinct, matchless in our unique strengths and abilities.

Whether you are single, married with no children or ten children, a stepmother, a grandmother, staying at home, or working three jobs just to get by . . . I pray you will be uplifted and strengthened by the message of this book. I pray that you will know that you are making a difference. You are important—to God, to your children, and to women everywhere who, day by day, are making the world a better place because they are mothers.

I AM A MOTHER

I'd rather be a mother than anyone on earth
Bringing up a child or two of unpretentious birth. . . .
I'd rather tuck a little child all safe and sound in bed
Than twine a chain of diamonds about my [carefree] head.
I'd rather wash a smudgy face with round, bright, baby eyes
Than paint the pageantry of fame or walk among the wise.

—Meredith Gray, from *The Beauty of Motherhood*

A couple of years ago, my husband and I attended a dinner meeting outside Washington, D.C. It was a wonderful gathering of about seventy-five mostly LDS couples from a variety of professions, including law, business, education, and communications. After dinner, each of us was asked to introduce him- or herself.

The men in the room confidently and appropriately stated their professional achievements, which were impressive. They had degrees; they served on boards; they tended to patients and served clients; they had accomplished sons and daughters.

Then their wives stood up—beautiful, intelligent, spiritual women. Many of them had served on boards, held degrees, and were seasoned in their respective fields. Each of them was also a mother.

But this is how many of the women described themselves:

"Oh, I'm just a mom."

"I don't have any credentials; I'm just raising our six children."

"My life's not very exciting right now; I'm just a stay-at-home mom."

"I don't have much to offer here. I'm just a mother."

We heard some variation of the phrase "I'm just a mother" repeated, almost apologetically, over and over again.

Their words surprised me. I had recently given birth to my first child, and I was on top of the world. My baby was a blessing that had come to me a little later in life than usual, and I was excited and honored to finally accept the mantle of motherhood. I felt an extraordinary sense of responsibility. And *power*. Not as the world defines the word, but from entering a sacred partnership with the Creator himself. What a remarkable gift! I wanted to shout from the rooftops, "I am a mother! I am a mother!"

So when I heard these women say, "I'm *just* a mother," I was taken aback. Was I missing something? Did these lovely women—these experienced mothers—know something I didn't? Was it simply a matter of time before I'd figure it out? Before I, too, would understand that motherhood was somehow of lesser importance?

I was so bewildered by their comments that questions began to gnaw at me—What have I done? *What have I done?*

When I left my television career in New York City to get married and to have a family, many of my colleagues told me I was crazy, that I was out of my mind. I had turned down a lucrative, four-year network contract, working on exciting, high-profile, prime-time projects.

Some people were incredibly supportive. One producer in particular came into my office, looked me straight in the eye, and said, "Good for you!" He wasn't endorsing my decision to be a mother *per se*, but he did congratulate me for having the courage to follow my heart, to act on my convictions. He noted that there were so very many others with the impulse to leave; but they wouldn't. They just couldn't walk away from the prestige, the money, or whatever it was that seemed more important than following their hearts.

By way of contrast, when I explained to another rather influential colleague that I would not be taking that contract offer, he told me I was making a terrible decision that I would regret for years to come. "What will you *be* without your job?" he asked. "If you leave television now, you're *done.*" He quoted an old CBS newsman as saying, "Without work, there is no meaning to life." And finally, knowing of my faith, he asked, "What are you going to do . . . move up there and teach Sunday School?" Well, as it turned out, the first Sunday in my new ward, I *was* called to teach—the Gospel Doctrine class.

I found that the reaction from my female colleagues was largely, and disappointingly, less than supportive. I shared my decision with one woman who smugly joked, "Why don't you just get a nanny?" Another network executive asked me what I was going to do once I got to Boston. I told her I was going to have a family, I was going to be a mother. "No, I understand that," she said, puzzled, "but what are you going to *do?*"

All of this was still fresh on my mind during that evening spent near Washington, D.C. A chorus of "I'm *just* a mother," juxtaposed with "What will you be without your job?" and "You're making a terrible mistake" made me wonder, *Could they be right?*

Is it possible that motherhood is an insignificant, second-rate occupation?

Had I made a bad decision? I thought I'd done everything right. I'd fasted and prayed. I'd felt such a powerful, spiritual confirmation that this was the right choice, for *me.* Could it be that Heavenly Father would *plan* for me to walk away from something I loved for the "misery" of being *"just* a mother"?

What I have since learned is that *God's* definition of motherhood and the *world's* definition are vastly different. And sometimes—probably all too often—the challenges, daily physical and emotional exhaustion, and occasional self-doubt that come along with being a mother cause many of us to buy into an inaccurate and destructive understanding of our role. There just doesn't seem to be a lot of joy—or fulfillment—associated with the world's interpretation of motherhood.

But when we trust in the arm of the Lord rather than the voices of the world, everything changes. Elder Neal A. Maxwell observed, "When the real history of mankind is fully disclosed, will it feature the echoes of gunfire or the shaping sound of lullabies? The great armistices made by military men or the peacemaking of women in homes and in neighborhoods? Will what happened in cradles and kitchens prove to be more controlling than what happened in congresses?" ("The Women of God," 10–11).

I see no "justs" when I read those words. Instead, I *feel* something: Honor. Responsibility. Awe. Hope. I begin to understand what the First Presidency of The Church of Jesus Christ of Latter-day Saints has been quietly reminding mothers for years, that "motherhood is near to divinity," the "highest, holiest service to be assumed by mankind" (J. Reuben Clark Jr., *Improvement Era*, 761).

At times, there may be few immediate rewards for those of us who are mothers. There are no Christmas bonuses, no promotions, no paid vacations. But there is love, there is laughter, there is joy. And there are assurances. For, as the Apostle Paul taught, "Eye hath not seen, nor ear heard, neither have entered into the heart of man, the things which God hath prepared for them that love him" (1 Corinthians 2:9). A mother who loves the Lord and teaches her children to do the same—above all else—cannot be denied this blessing.

President Gordon B. Hinckley has said, "God planted within women something divine" (*Teachings of Gordon B. Hinckley,* 387). It is that divinity that makes women nurturers, that encourages a woman to pursue motherhood—even when that means sacrificing her own comforts for those of her children . . . and loving those children with a fierceness and loyalty that is incomparable.

What power we would possess if every mother would turn off the voices of the world and instead truly believe what

President Hinckley and all the prophets have taught—and the Lord has promised!

Changing the Way We Think

Sometimes, if you listen for it, you *can* find voices in the world that echo President Hinckley's words. I love it when I hear educated, talented, well-known women from different corridors of life call on other women to raise the image of motherhood, to erase the feeling that any of us are "just mothers." Recently, I watched an interview with Maria Shriver, the wife of California Governor Arnold Schwarzenegger. She was explaining her agenda as the state's first lady and said that one of her goals is to "empower mothers"!

"How do we get women," she said, "to stop saying, 'I'm *just* a mother.' Or, 'I *used* to be such and such, but now I'm *just* a mother? We need to market motherhood. So I came up with a saying: 'Motherhood: 24/7 on the frontlines of humanity. Are you man enough to try it?'" (from "First Lady Maria Shriver— Her New Life," *The Oprah Winfrey Show,* April 29, 2004).

"In our society, we give motherhood plenty of lip service," says Oprah Winfrey, another champion of motherhood. "We pat moms on the head, bring them flowers on Mother's Day, and honor them before crowds. But at the end of the day, we don't extend them the same respect we would a professor, a dentist, an accountant, or a judge.

"I believe the choice to become a mother is the choice to become one of the greatest spiritual teachers there is. To create an environment that's stimulating and nurturing, to pass on a sense of responsibility to another human being, to raise a child who understands that he or she is created from good and is capable of anything—I know for sure that few callings are more honorable. To play down mothering as small is to crack the very foundation on which greatness stands.

"The world can only value mothering to the extent that women everywhere *stand and declare that it must be so.* In our hands we hold the power to transform the perception of mother-hood. . . . We should no longer allow a mother to be defined as 'just a mom.' It is on her back that great nations are built" ("What I Know for Sure," *O, The Oprah Magazine,* 66; emphasis added).

Sister Sheri Dew adds a spiritual component to that thought:

"It's no wonder," she says, "that Satan has declared war on motherhood. He knows that those who rock the cradle can rock his earthly empire. And he knows that without righteous moth-ers loving and leading the next generation, the kingdom of God will fail. When we understand the magnitude of motherhood, it becomes clear why prophets have been so protective of woman's most sacred role" ("Are We Not All Mothers?" *Ensign*, 96).

Are you protective of that role? When asked, do you meekly respond that you're *"just* a mother," or do you confidently declare, "I am a mother"?

True Success

I recently met with a group of beautiful high-school-aged young women. The Young Women president asked these impressive girls to describe what they wanted to "be" when they grew up, and the girls spent some time responding:

"I want to be a veterinarian."

"I want to be an artist."

"I want to be a figure skater."

This pattern continued around the room.

Then, one young woman raised her hand and shyly, as if she were embarrassed to admit it, said, "I've always wanted to be a mother."

One of my friends recently shared an experience she'd had with a thirteen-year-old in her neighborhood. This bright, talented young woman often stops by my friend's house on the way home from school to talk about her day and just hang out.

One afternoon, their conversation turned to motherhood, and this girl told my friend, "I want to have only one child when

I grow up, because I want to be more than just a mom and sit on the couch all day."

General Young Women President Susan W. Tanner has related several similar experiences with beautiful young girls who, when asked what they want to be, have been hesitant—even fearful—to express their desires to be mothers. And with other girls who have emphatically declared that they want to be more than *just* mothers.

Sister Tanner's own daughter has stated that "one of the disturbing anxieties in her life" is the lack of affirmation motherhood receives on all fronts—at school, at Young Women activities, even at seminary (see "Strengthening Future Mothers," 20).

Sisters, we must revere motherhood in our homes, in our church callings, in our places of employment, in our associations with our neighbors, in everything we do. If we do not, what are we teaching our daughters? How can we expect the rising generation of young women to enthusiastically embrace *their* futures as mothers and leaders if we are ambivalent or apologetic about our own motherhood?

When mothers themselves begin to revere their callings, so much can change. And surely, when a woman of virtue values motherhood above other pursuits, her children will "arise up, and call her blessed" (Proverbs 31:28).

Still, the sanctity of motherhood can be hard to appreciate when you spend endless hours making peanut butter and jelly sandwiches, singing along with Elmo, helping create elaborate science projects, or enforcing late-night curfews. Many in the world will shout that motherhood is full of small, mundane tasks. And certainly, if you look only on the surface, this is true. But underneath all of the secondary things mothers do—cook, clean, read, chauffeur, nurse, and so on—is a mother's real occupation and, I believe, the definition of true success. Webster defines *occupation* as "the principal business of one's life." The principal business of a mother's life is loving and nurturing her children; it is teaching them, by example, how to pass on that love and thereby strengthening the world around them.

For years, many in the business world have taught—and been taught—that the definition of success is *achievement*, chiefly in career and financial terms. At the Harvard Business School, the model of success included one word: *achievement*. A few years ago, however, Harvard took another look at the model and added a few more words: *happiness, significance*, and *legacy*. Is there any other person who can bring more happiness to her young charges, has more significance in another's life, or has the potential to leave a greater legacy for those who come after her than a mother?

I believe, from the depths of my heart, that a righteous

mother is the embodiment of success. I believed this about motherhood before I got married and had children. Now, I *know* it: As a woman, the most important work I will ever do will happen within the walls of my own home.

Having said that, I must admit that there are some days when I think it would be easier, if not preferable, to be a foreign correspondent than to be a mother. There are definitely moments when I am down on my hands and knees, mopping up yet another mess, when I look up at the TV to see one of my old friends interviewing someone famous or globe-trotting on a big story, and I think, *What have I done?* But as I look at the little faces of my children, I realize I would not trade in my current occupation. Not for anything.

I know what I gave up so that I could be a mother during this season of my life. But I also know what I gave it up for. I traded in fancy lunches in fancy restaurants for rice cereal and bunny-shaped macaroni and cheese. There's no one to do my hair and makeup anymore. Some mornings I'm lucky to squeeze in a shower. When I get up at 4:00 A.M. these days, it's not to be chauffeured to a television studio. Instead, you'll find me huddled near a nightlight, lulling a little baby (or two!) back to sleep. No more pats on the back for booking exclusive interviews. They don't give awards for best diaper change of the day.

And I don't get a paycheck that can be cashed at any bank. Now my compensation comes in packages money can't buy.

Indeed, every mother who prayerfully chooses her own path in life—no matter where that path leads—does not have to apologize for being a mother. As she loves her children, as she sacrifices—in her own way and within her own capabilities— she will be led by the Savior and buoyed up by his loving care as she works to rear "the offspring" of God (Acts 17:28). In this, she will have acquired true success.

A Mother's Influence

When I was pregnant with Ella, I started a little stitchery project (which I will someday finish!). It's a quote from the book of Alma, in the Book of Mormon: "They had been *taught by their mothers,* that if they did not doubt, God would deliver them. And they rehearsed unto me the words of their mothers, saying: *We do not doubt our mothers knew it*" (Alma 56:47–48; emphasis added).

Can you imagine the joy experienced by the mothers of Helaman's 2,000 stripling warriors? Can you imagine how it must have felt to know that it was their teachings and their testimonies that gave their sons the courage and faith to honor sacred covenants under extraordinarily difficult circumstances? Mothers today can expect similar challenges and potential success as we work to raise another army of righteous youth. I strive to be like those faithful mothers and to one day be able to say, "I have no greater joy than to hear that my children walk in truth" (3 John 1:4).

President David O. McKay once said of women: "She who can paint a masterpiece or write a book that will influence millions deserves the admiration and the plaudits of mankind; but she who rears successfully a family of healthy, beautiful sons and daughters, whose influence will be felt through generations to come, . . . long after paintings shall have faded, and books and statues shall have decayed or shall have been destroyed, deserves the highest honor that man can give, and the choicest blessings of God. In her high duty and service to humanity . . . , she is co-partner with the Creator himself" (*Gospel Ideals*, 453–54).

A Co-partner with the Creator Himself

I felt that relationship in a very profound way after the birth of our second child. We were sitting in church on the Sunday after Thanksgiving, when my water broke. Three days later, our little baby William was born—more than three months early, at only twenty-seven weeks gestation. At his tiniest, he weighed just over two and a half pounds.

I remember the nurses wheeling me on a bed into the Neonatal Intensive Care Unit at Brigham and Women's Hospital in Boston to see him for the first time. It was four o'clock in the morning, and I had just awakened from undergoing a difficult and complicated two-and-a-half-hour caesarean section operation.

I saw all those little incubators—with blankets covering them to keep the light out of the babies' eyes—and thought they looked like little coffins lined up.

How could these babies survive? Of course, some of them didn't.

William was in the NICU for eleven weeks. Almost every day, I would travel back and forth to that hospital to deliver breast milk and to hold him. Some days the doctors would not allow him to come out of the Isolette. And so I would sit and look at him through the glass, with all the tape and tubes and wires hanging from his frail little body. There was barely a place to touch his bare skin.

On the good days, I would hold William while he received his fortified feedings through a tube in his nose. I had read medical research that showed that premature babies who were consistently held and nurtured by their mothers were healthier than those who were not. The hospital recommended "kangaroo care"—putting babies skin-to-skin with their mothers. It was supposed to help with bonding. The doctors said it actually made the babies stronger.

For weeks, I did this. But for weeks it seemed that William still did not know I was there. He didn't respond to me in any way. He didn't open his eyes. He would hardly move. I remember so distinctly thinking: *Am I really making a difference?*

A very perceptive neonatologist must have sensed my sadness. One afternoon, she came over to our little corner of the unit, put her arm around me, and with such kindness said, "William can't express it right now, but in his behalf, let me say *Thank You* for being here. These babies *know* their mothers. And even though it doesn't feel as though you're making a difference . . . *you are.*"

That night, after my husband had given William a beautiful priesthood blessing, I remember standing with both arms through the portals of his incubator. The feeling came over me so strongly that as a mother, the Lord needed *me.* And that, as my Savior, I needed Him to make this baby whole. In that moment, in a very tangible way, I realized that mothers matter.

Even when our children cannot—or *will not*—express it, even when the voices of the world tell us that mothering isn't as important as anything else we could be doing, *we are making a difference.*

I keep this quote from Elder Jeffrey R. Holland taped to my nightstand: "You are doing God's work. You are doing it wonderfully well. He is blessing you, and He will bless you, even—no, especially—when your days and your nights may be most challenging. Like the woman who anonymously, meekly, perhaps even with hesitation and some embarrassment, fought her way through the crowd just to touch the hem of the Master's garment, so Christ will say to the women who worry and wonder and weep over their responsibility as mothers, 'Daughter, be of good comfort; thy faith hath made thee whole.' And it will make your children whole as well" ("Because She Is a Mother," 37).

A "co-partner with the Creator himself."

That is a mother.

We are mothers.

The next time someone inquires what you do or asks you to describe yourself, would you say with confidence and with joy, "I am a Mother"?

chapter two

A Pencil in the Hand of God— My Story

Most forms of holding back are rooted in pride or are prompted by the mistaken notion that somehow we are diminished by submission to God. Actually, the greater the submission, the greater the expansion!

—Neal A. Maxwell, *On Becoming a Disciple-Scholar*, 22

When I was in college, I cut out a wonderful article from *Time* magazine. It wasn't a splashy cover story or a glossy two-page spread. In fact, it was buried between advertisements for fancy watches and expensive cars. If you didn't look closely, you might have missed the headline.

The article was an interview with Mother Teresa. It wasn't

long, but it was very profound. She talked about her mission to
bring peace and happiness to the impoverished and suffering in
Calcutta. At one point, the reporter asked the Nobel Peace Prize
winner to describe herself.

This is what she said:

"I am like a little pencil in [God's] hand. That is all. He does
the thinking. He does the writing. The pencil has nothing to do
with it. The pencil has only to be allowed to be used" ("Mother
Teresa: Missionary of Compassion," *Time*, December 4, 1989).

A pencil in the hand of God—such a simple yet eloquent way
to describe what I truly believe is one of the most important
principles in the gospel of Jesus Christ: submitting to his will so
the Spirit can guide our lives.

The scriptures are full of examples of men and women who
learned to submit to God's will. At the beginning of the Book of
Mormon, Nephi promises his father, Lehi, "I will go and do the
things which the Lord hath commanded" (1 Nephi 3:7). Alma
states that true discipleship means being "led by the Holy Spirit,
becoming humble, meek, submissive, patient, full of love and all
long-suffering" (Alma 13:28).

In the New Testament, we get a glimpse of the prophetess
Anna, who chose to devote her life to God's will, serving the
Lord "night and day" (Luke 2:37). In section 25 of the Doctrine
and Covenants, we read of the Lord's promise to Emma Smith if

she is obedient: "Thou shalt be ordained under [Joseph Smith's] hand to expound scriptures, and to exhort the church, according as it shall be given thee by my Spirit" (v. 7). Twelve years after this revelation, Emma became the first president of the Church's female Relief Society.

And, of course, the Savior himself "suffered the will of the Father" to the extent of sacrificing his own life. This is what he said when he appeared to the Nephites: "I am Jesus Christ, whom the prophets testified shall come into the world. . . . I am the light and the life of the world; and I have drunk out of that bitter cup which the Father hath given me, and have glorified the Father in taking upon me the sins of the world, in the which I have suffered the will of the Father in all things from the beginning" (3 Nephi 11:10–11).

Of the Savior's visit to the Nephites, Elder Jeffrey R. Holland said: "I cannot think it either accident or mere whimsy that the Good Shepherd in his newly exalted state, appearing to a most significant segment of his flock, chooses to speak first of his *obedience, his deference, his loyalty, and loving submission to his Father.* In an initial and profound moment of spellbinding wonder, when surely he has the attention of every man, woman, and child as far as the eye can see, his submission to his Father is the first and most important thing he wishes us to know about himself.

"Frankly, I am a bit haunted by the thought that this is the first and most important thing he may want to know about *us* when we meet him one day in similar fashion. Did we obey, even if it was painful? Did we submit, even if the cup was bitter indeed?" (*On Earth As It Is in Heaven*, 126; emphasis added).

I often think about Elder Holland's statement and wonder,

Will the Lord look upon me one day and see an obedient servant? Will he see a woman who was willing to be a pencil in the hand of God, to do his work humbly and happily, even when it was painful or difficult?

As I look back on my life, personally and professionally, I see with clarity how the Lord *has* guided me. And although the story he has written for me is completely different from the version I had in my own mind, I know now that his plan is better for me than the one I had mapped out for myself.

Oh, but at times, it has been painful.

My Story

I arrived at the doorstep of Tingey Hall on the campus of Brigham Young University in the fall of 1985. I was so excited to be there—and to begin living the life I had planned. In fact, I had a very detailed outline, a precise time line, for myself—and for the Lord! The wedding colors were set (peach and teal). My dress was picked out (*McCall's* pattern #7847). And I'd compiled a list of baby names (Lauren, Sydney, or Elizabeth for a girl; Matthew, Ryan, or David for a boy).

The plan was pretty straightforward . . . easily executed, I thought: I'd graduate in April, get married in August, have a baby a year from December. Then, I'd get pregnant every two to three years until I had five kids. I would teach violin lessons on the side, volunteer for the PTA, serve in the Church, and settle down into a quiet, fulfilling life.

Okay, I informed the Lord, *I'm ready to go!*

Well, you can imagine my shock and sense of disappointment when things didn't go quite as I had planned. I watched with great sadness—and some fear—as roommates and girlfriends, one after the next, found their companions, had babies, and began living the life I had planned for myself.

I'll never forget the day I graduated from BYU in 1990. It was April, all right. But there was little hope for an August wedding. In fact, it didn't appear that *any* wedding was on the horizon. I remember walking off campus with a diploma tucked in my purse, feeling completely panicked. My parents wanted to take me out to celebrate, so we drove to Salt Lake City for dinner. We got as far as the stoplight in front of Liberty Park on 900 South when it hit me like a brick: *What am I going to do now?*

Had I known back then what was ahead of me, good and bad, I'm not sure I would have ever gotten out of that car!

I never set out to have a career in television news. In fact, I started college on a music scholarship, playing the violin in the philharmonic and chamber orchestras. I made my way through the English department and the Elementary Education department before finally ending up at the campus radio station, writing thirty-second news and weather cut-ins for KBYU-FM. I loved it. But I still felt that I was merely filling time until my "real" life kicked in.

In 1989, while I was still in college, I was hired as a part-time, Saturday reporter at KSL Television in Salt Lake City. Some weeks after graduation, I was offered a full-time position at the station as a general assignment reporter. A couple of my old professors seemed genuinely surprised to learn that I was working in television. They knew of the plans I had for myself and were quite aware that none of those plans included a "real job" in TV.

At KSL, I was the new kid, right out of school. That didn't go over so well with many of the very talented, veteran journalists who, frankly, didn't think I belonged there, that I had yet to earn a place in the newsroom. Looking back, I think they were probably right. I figured out very quickly that I was on a pretty steep learning curve. I needed help.

So one day, at the end of my reporting shift, I approached someone I respected, who I thought might be able to give me a few good pointers, an honest critique, and some professional advice about my writing and on-air delivery. Right there, in front of the assignment desk, I asked him, simply, if he would help me. He looked me straight in the eye and said, "I'm here to produce a broadcast, not train *you!*"

Hmmm . . . another "Now what?" moment.

Well, I first headed straight for the ladies' room for a good, long cry. Then, a few days later, I tried again. This time, I went to the executive producer at the station, a step up from my last attempt, a woman with much more experience and—more important—a willingness to share it.

The first thing she did was walk me into an edit room with a stack of tapes, a yellow notepad, and a long list of recommendations, things I needed to do to improve.

Over time she became much like a mother and a mentor to me, guiding and shaping me with a gentle hand but always allowing me the freedom to make my own mistakes.

That was the beginning. I was young, had only a little experience, and was still unsure about the unexpected path my life was taking; this route certainly didn't exist in the script I had outlined five years earlier. But with each day, I learned. And bit by bit, I began to allow the Lord to guide my hand as I settled into this new career.

More Change

Then, one day in late 1995, I received a call from an agent in New York City. He had seen my work on a videotape sent to him by another reporter who was trying to get a job in a bigger market. Within a few weeks, I had traveled to New York for interviews and had been hired by ABC News to anchor a twenty-four-hour cable news channel, based in Los Angeles. It was a start-up operation, designed to compete with NBC's MSNBC, which is still on the air today. By this time, my revised script *did* include a career in television, and I was excited to venture into network news.

It was also during this time that one of my lifelong dreams seemed to finally be coming into focus: shortly before moving to L.A., I had gotten married. My husband lived and worked outside L.A., so this new job opportunity seemed perfect: I would work for a short time and then settle down and start a family. Everything appeared to be back on track. I started out on this new adventure hopeful that I might get to revisit part of my original script, never imagining that it would require significant additional (even painful) revisions.

The first revision came on the very day I arrived in Los Angeles. I opened the *Los Angeles Times* to read a headline that literally took my breath away. There it was: "ABC Cancels Plans for Cable News."

To say I was shocked is an understatement. Can you imagine getting this type of news from the newspaper? What did it mean? Would I lose my contract? Would ABC keep me but insist I move to New York? Was there a possibility that this might be my chance to just walk away and start the family I wanted so much? Could this actually be a good thing?

Well, it turned out that ABC *did* want to honor my contract—and they let me stay in L.A. So, on the day I was supposed to start work in cable news, I showed up at ABC's Los Angeles Bureau instead, ready to cover any story they would offer.

Unfortunately, there were no stories to be had . . . none at all. So, for several weeks, I just sat there . . . and sat there . . . and sat there, wondering what was going to happen in my life and where doing nothing would lead me.

Finally, one day I decided I couldn't take it anymore. I got on the telephone and began telling everyone who would listen at ABC that I wanted to contribute, something, *anything*.

Looking back, I see that I was pretty relentless—and, I'm sure, quite a nuisance. But I kept at it, determined to turn my disappointment into success. Finally, the bureau chief appeared at my desk one morning and handed me a piece of paper with instructions for my first official assignment: "Camp O.J. 8:00 tomorrow morning."

For the next five months, I prepared for—and then covered—the O. J. Simpson civil trial—reporting on the air for *Good Morning America.*

With just a little glitch in my new and revised plan, things were off to a better start.

For a while.

Professionally, I was on a roll—getting good stories, making great contacts, and enjoying my work. Personally, however, life wasn't going quite as planned. Though all the elements of my script were present, the events I had dreamed of weren't taking place. Despite my prayers, my faith, and my willingness to persevere, this became one of the most difficult periods of my life as my marriage began to fail.

I felt as if I were lost at the bottom of a great hole deep in the earth, rather than on top of the world, where I had hoped to be by this time in my life.

Only after much prayer and heartache and self-examination, I realized the marriage was over.

I was, indeed, broken in a way; but I wasn't without hope. I still had faith in my Savior and his atoning sacrifice, his ability to heal my heart and show me how to start anew, to move forward and do his work—in a way only he knew I was capable of doing.

And so I persevered and prayed some more. I continued to

work. I found happiness in the light of the gospel and in my relationships with my family and friends.

A High-Stakes Venture

In August of 1999, nearly fifteen years after I had submitted my "original script" to the Lord, I was hired by CBS News to coanchor with Bryant Gumbel a morning network television program called *The Early Show.* CBS had spent decades competing against two very strong morning broadcasts at ABC and NBC and was ready to roll out a new format and new anchors in a multi-million dollar, state-of-the-art studio on 5th Avenue in the heart of New York City.

It was a high-stakes venture, with high pressure and high expectations.

Just a few days before my departure for New York, I was scurrying around my little studio apartment on the outskirts of Los Angeles, frantically making lists of everything I still needed to do, when the telephone rang.

My jaw fell to the floor as the voice on the other end of the line explained: "This is Elder Neal Maxwell's office in Salt Lake City. Elder Maxwell would like to speak with you. Do you have a moment that I may put him on the line?" Suddenly, there was nothing on my to-do list but to speak with an apostle of the Lord.

Elder Maxwell was gracious and kind. He briefly explained that in his capacity overseeing Church Public Affairs, he had heard about my new opportunity in New York. He told me he felt prompted to offer me a blessing as I began this new chapter in my life. If I was interested, he said, and if it wasn't too "inconvenient," perhaps I could pass through Salt Lake City on my way to New York.

I hung up the phone and immediately changed my flight plans. Within a few days, my parents and I flew to Salt Lake and drove to Elder Maxwell's home. He and Sister Maxwell welcomed us so warmly—as if we had known them for years.

As he pronounced the blessing, I was struck by his extraordinary eloquence. The Spirit was so powerful. Elder Maxwell said many things, but there was one directive that penetrated my mind most deeply: "You must allow the Lord to use you. . . . Sometimes you will not understand what he is doing . . . or why he is doing it. But do not question. You must allow him to *guide* you and *direct* you."

It seems that the stakes were even higher than I had imagined.

Sister Maxwell served us delicious soda cracker peach pie and, less than an hour after we had arrived, we were back at the airport boarding our connecting flight to New York.

We arrived in the city, and my parents stayed with me for a

few days to get me settled. The night after they left was terrifying. I was lonely and very much afraid. I vividly remember sitting alone in my apartment, looking out over the Hudson River, from thirty stories up, and feeling like I might as well be on the surface of Mars. Everything felt so foreign to me. *Can I really do this?* I thought. *Am I good enough?* And, in the back of my mind, part of me wondered, *Have I just left behind the last chance I'll get to play out the life I had scripted for myself so many years ago?*

Clearly, the pencil needed more sharpening.

As the night wore on, I thought about Elder Maxwell's words and the spirit of his blessing: "Allow the Lord to use you. . . . You may not understand what he is doing or why he is doing it. Just allow him to use you." I was being encouraged, directed really, to be a pencil in the hand of God. My script was being rewritten, revised by hands more capable than my own.

Within a few days, I found myself at the center of a conference call. And I began to understand, just a little bit, some of what was ahead. It was actually a press conference, via telephone. I was being "introduced" as the new co-anchor of *The Early Show*. Twenty to thirty print reporters from around the country had gathered from their respective cities. They were journalists and critics from newspapers and magazines such as the *Los Angeles Times*, *The New York Times*, *USA Today*, *People*, and *TV Guide*. It was a tough crowd.

I remember a conversation with the president of CBS News just before the call. We were reviewing "talking points" for this important meeting, and I told him I had a feeling that my religion might come up in the course of the conference call.

In a somewhat disbelieving tone he said, "Oh, Jane, we're *beyond* that."

Well, sure enough, not more than three minutes into the conference call, came one of the first questions. It wasn't about my reporting experience. It wasn't about any stories I'd covered. It had to do with my choice of *beverage* in the morning. They could not believe that I didn't drink coffee!

One female reporter nearly shouted out, in a deep, gruff voice: "You're a Mormon?"

"Yes, I am."

"Do you drink coffee?"

"No, no, I don't drink coffee." Slight pause . . .

"How can anyone possibly wake up at 3:45 in the morning, do a two-hour television broadcast, and *not drink coffee?*"

I began laughing but soon realized that she wasn't kidding.

The next morning, her newspaper column read something like this: "Jane Clayson . . . a Mormon who doesn't drink coffee . . . " and on with the rest of the story.

Anchoring *The Early Show* was one of the most invigorating experiences of my life. It was also one of the most difficult periods of my life because of the physically and emotionally grueling routine it required. I had absolutely no idea what I was getting myself into.

Mornings began with that 3:45 A.M. alarm clock. I'd arrive at the 5th Avenue studio and, depending on how big the bags were under my eyes, spend thirty to forty minutes in hair and makeup. Stop off in wardrobe. Skim four newspapers. Revise and prepare news segments for that day. Be briefed by producers about overnight interview changes. Be on the air at 6:30 A.M. to promote the broadcast to five or six East Coast affiliate, local-station anchor teams. Cameras were live from 7:00 to 9:00 A.M. There was more promotion with West Coast anchors until 10:00 A.M. Then we often updated the program during breaking news . . .

And that was the fun part of the day.

Following the show, meetings lasted until noon. Luncheons or speaking engagements at midday. There was almost always a story shoot or a taped interview to be done in the afternoon. I'd get home by 5:30 P.M. for a quick dinner. And then packets would arrive between 6:30 and 7:00 P.M. Packets meant *homework*. Lots of homework. Preparation for the next day's show included reading, outlining, and preparing questions from five 15- to 20-page information packets. I used to say it was like preparing for five college-level term papers every night.

Bedtime was 9:00 or maybe 9:30. And then it was time to get up and do it all over again.

The routine was relentless. But every morning brought an opportunity to interview the biggest newsmakers of the day, from Washington, D.C., to Hollywood and all around the world. It was the Secretary of State one minute, Martha Stewart the next.

And more often than I ever imagined, some issue related to my religion would come up. Not only did I not take a morning coffee, but I also had to explain to producers that I needed sparkling cider on the set in lieu of the wine or champagne everybody else was drinking during cooking segments (yes, it was 8:30 in the morning!).

I soon realized that *who* I was and *what* I believed was a source of fascination for some people. So what I *said* and how I *reacted* was always very much in the forefront of my mind.

I met many people and interacted with many colleagues who, surprisingly, would say to me, "I've never met a Mormon before." In the world of network news I was an anomaly. I sometimes felt like a display in a department store window and heard more than once, "Oh, *you're* the Mormon!"

There were many wonderful opportunities to move beyond the inevitable questions about polygamy and the Word of Wisdom and help people understand Latter-day Saints as people of faith and service who live good lives and try to do what's right. In a very profound way, I felt a special responsibility as a member of the Lord's Church. And as time went on I could feel myself being used as a pencil in the hand of God, writing a chapter in my life that I never could have imagined.

Still, there were plenty of powerful and persuasive voices trying to nudge me into doing things that would have made up a very different kind of story.

I remember, in particular, a lunch meeting with a CBS executive who handed me a "personal PR plan" in conjunction with the broadcast. As part of that plan she suggested that it would be very nice if I dated someone "famous, maybe an actor or an athlete," she said. "That's always a sure way to generate good press."

Sure, good press for the show, but what would it do to my story, the one I had been slowly turning over to the Lord?

Looking for More

As the days went by, my college years seemed like a dream from an eternity before. I imagined that the script I had written fifteen years earlier, but still never acted out, was going to continue to collect dust as I followed a different path, one with its own challenges and rewards. Then a poignant moment initiated a series of events that changed the course of my life.

I was at Ground Zero in New York City on the one-year

anniversary of the September 11, 2001, terrorist attacks on our country, anchoring, with Dan Rather, CBS's coverage of that terrible day. I had returned from Washington, D.C., two days earlier, where I had interviewed First Lady Laura Bush in the Blue Room of the White House. In many ways, professionally, I was on top of the world.

But I vividly felt a certain emptiness.

The emotions of the day hit me quite forcefully. I looked into the faces of those who had lost someone the year before—a husband, wife, mother, father, brother, sister, best friend—and thought, over and over, *Life is so fragile. The most important things we have are our relationships with our families and those we love.*

I could not put those feelings aside. As I allowed my mind to wander and reflect, I stumbled upon two quotes that have since become favorites:

First, from the actress and comedienne Lily Tomlin: "You can win the rat race, but you're still a rat."

And this, from the Pulitzer-Prize-winning writer Anna Quindlen: "If your success is not on your own terms, if it looks good to the world but *does not feel good in your soul*, it is not success at all" (*Loud and Clear*, 212; emphasis added).

It hit me that there will always be another project. There will always be another interview. There will always be another high-profile assignment. Make no mistake, I *was* grateful for the many tremendous experiences I was having. I *was* passionate about my work. I even felt that I was fulfilling a particular mission I had been called to serve. But I also felt that one of my deepest longings had not been met. And that was to be a wife and a mother.

Shortly after this experience, I met my husband, Mark. And, not long after, on the grounds of the Salt Lake Temple, he asked me to marry him. Seven weeks later we returned to the Salt Lake Temple, where we were married.

By this time, I knew better than to question any changes in the script. What happened over the course of the next few months is not something I could have choreographed on my own, or even dreamed up for that matter. In fact, I am convinced that the timing of some of the events that followed were more than interesting coincidences. As Elder David A. Bednar has testified, the Lord's timing and his tender mercies "are real and that they do not occur randomly or merely by coincidence. Often, the Lord's timing of His tender mercies helps us to both discern and acknowledge them" ("The Tender Mercies of the Lord," 99).

More Than a Coincidence

Mark proposed to me on a Thursday night at about 8:00 P.M. The next day, Friday morning, not less than twelve hours later, I got a call from my long-time agent in New York City. He was very excited. With my contract expiring at CBS News, he was calling to tell me that he had brokered a deal for me—a lucrative, four-year network contract, working in New York City, on some very interesting and exciting projects. At that moment, it could not have been more clear to me that the Lord was laying out two very distinct choices, two vastly different paths.

For weeks, Mark and I prayed about this. We weighed the pros and cons of this wonderful, yet very demanding opportunity that would bring with it long hours and lots of travel. What would it mean for our family? And what would it mean for me to potentially walk away?

I thought a lot about who I was and who I wanted to become. I wondered if leaving my career would one day make me look back and feel that some part of me was lost, never to return. I wondered if *staying* in my career would prevent me from realizing one of my greatest dreams. I thought of that quote again: "If it looks good to the world but does not feel good in your soul, it is not success at all." I couldn't help wondering, *Will taking this new opportunity ultimately feel good in my soul?*

I had some very real fears. I also had some of the strongest promptings and some of the most powerful spiritual moments of my life. Instead of thinking about who *I* wanted to become, I started thinking about what *God* would have me become. What was his plan for me?

Finally, I decided to leave New York City and the world of

network news. When I did that, I recognized I might not simply be putting my career *on hold.*

I reflected often on these words of Elder Holland: "In those crucial moments of pivotal personal history [we must] submit ourselves to God even when all our hopes and fears may tempt us otherwise. We must be willing to place *all* that we have—not just our possessions . . . but also our ambition and pride and stubbornness and vanity—on the altar of God, kneel there in silent submission, and willingly walk away" (*On Earth As It Is in Heaven,* 128; emphasis in original).

It takes a great deal of faith to do that, whatever the circumstance. But I can tell you, the rewards are exquisite.

That first workday after my CBS contract expired, after I had moved to Boston and Mark and I had settled in, I will admit that I was a little nervous. After fifteen years and a very different pace of life, how would I feel? It was on *that* day that I found out Mark and I were expecting a child. Another coincidence? I don't think so. The Lord, in his love and tender mercy, sends signs and confirmations in the most wonderful ways.

This experience has taught me one of the most important lessons of my life, which I feel impressed to share, often, especially with young women: *There are seasons in life.* Don't ever let anyone deny you the blessings and joy of one season because they believe you should *be in*—or *stay in*—another season.

And never—never—be afraid to aspire to be a mother. Get your education. Go have experiences now that will broaden your mind and enrich you as a person. But don't forget what is most important.

Although marriage and motherhood didn't come to me when I planned, they did come . . . after years of prayer and faith and learning to submit to God's will, to become "a little pencil in his hand."

I have learned, as Elder Maxwell has so eloquently taught, that "the submission of one's will is placing on God's altar the *only uniquely personal thing one has to place there*. The many other things we 'give' are actually the things He has already given or loaned to us. However, when we finally submit ourselves by letting our individual wills be swallowed up in God's will, we will really be giving something to Him! It is the only possession which is truly ours to give" (*If Thou Endure It Well*, 54; emphasis added).

I still have a passion for broadcasting. I still consider myself a journalist—and I take in a project every once in a while. I don't know when the next season will begin or where it will take me.

But I *do* know this: I am a mother.

And it "feels good in my soul."

chapter three

WHY IT MATTERS

*If we stop to think about what we do, really do, we are
building for the centuries. We are building character, and
tradition, and values, which meander like a river into the
distance and out of our sight, but on and on and on.*

—Anna Quindlen, *Loud and Clear,* 57

After my husband, Mark, was baptized and confirmed a
member of the Church at age thirty-six, the bishop asked him to
stand before the congregation and bear his testimony. Mark
remembers the Spirit flooding his soul, washing over every part
of him, as he walked to the front of the chapel. When he finally
stood at the pulpit and looked out over the congregation, the

first face he saw was his mother's. An overwhelming feeling of gratitude filled his heart. He bore witness of the truthfulness of the gospel; and then he thanked his mother. She is not a member of the Church; but she is the reason that Mark was able to feel the Spirit and know that the Church is true. Her faith in God, her belief in the Bible as holy scripture, her witness—and example—that prayer really works had imprinted itself on Mark's heart as a young boy and helped lead him to the waters of baptism.

Mothers Are Powerful

So why is it that, while most of us honor our own mothers, society as a whole doesn't always seem to appreciate—or even understand—what being a mother entails or how much of an impact mothers have on our families, communities, and nations?

Why don't we honor motherhood more? Why don't we mother with more delight? Why do we seem to struggle so much with the value of this great calling? Do we really understand its significance and get it that the seemingly small things we do while our children are young—teaching them to pray, reading them a story, telling them how much we love them—tend to stick with them throughout life?

Why *do* mothers matter?

A recent editorial in *USA Today* reflected on the nation's inability to agree on the value of motherhood: "Society is deeply ambivalent about mothers. Yes, the idealistic Hallmark take on motherhood is deeply rooted: the selfless woman who bakes apple pies, loves her children unconditionally, and so on. But ever since the 1960s, the feminist movement has introduced another scale of measurement: Women should become CEOs, lawmakers, and astronauts like men. And pull in earnings to match" ("Hey Mom, You're Underpaid," *USA Today*, May 5, 2005).

These dual expectations are tough to live up to. And even on our best days, it's hard for a mom to believe that spending an hour scrubbing apple juice off the floor (and the walls, the refrigerator, and every other tiny crevice that a spilled cup of juice is capable of reaching!) is tantamount to setting public policy or breaking national news.

Perhaps you can relate to a conversation I had recently.

Party guest: "What do you do?"

Me: "I am a mother."

Audible pause. "Oh, congratulations . . ."

End of conversation.

My inquisitor on this occasion quickly moved on, having summed me up, perhaps, as less interesting than the next party guest. Maybe that same person would have been more motivated to keep talking if my response had been, "I'm a network news anchor for CBS," or, "I'm a foreign correspondent at ABC."

My experience is certainly not isolated.

Former *New York Times* reporter and Pulitzer Prize nominee Ann Crittenden writes: "Any woman who has devoted herself to raising children has experienced the hollow praise that only thinly conceals smug dismissal. In a culture that measures worth and achievement almost solely in terms of money, the intensive work of rearing responsible adults counts for little. One of the most intriguing questions in economic history is how this came to be; how mothers came to be excluded from the ranks of productive citizens. How did the demanding job of rearing a modern child come to be trivialized as baby-sitting? When did caring for children become a 'labor of love,' smothered under a blanket of sentimentality that hides its economic importance?" (*The Price of Motherhood*, 45).

Indeed, why is it that in this day and age there are so many who think so little of motherhood?

In her book, *We Are Our Mothers' Daughters*, journalist Cokie Roberts describes, in part, how this happened:

"For most of human history, men and women worked together in the same place and each one's work complemented the other's. No one thought the farmer's job was more important than the farmer's wife's. Neither could manage without the other. . . .

"It was the industrial revolution that changed everything. Men went out to work for wages, and they were paid for the hours they put in, not the tasks they completed. . . . Suddenly, what women did at home lost its value because there was no paycheck attached. Repetitive housework replaced home manufacture as women's crafts moved into assembly-line production. And that's what we've been struggling with ever since.

"Doing work that is economically rewarded and socially recognized means leaving home. . . . Women aren't paid for their jobs as nurturers" (222–24).

Do You Remember Who You Are?

A couple of summers ago, my husband had business in Asia and asked if I would join him for several weeks.

One weekend, we traveled to Hanoi, Vietnam, and visited the tomb of Ho Chi Minh. Standing in line in front of us was a woman from Bethesda, Maryland. We seemed to be the only Americans around, and we quickly began chatting about the sites, the scorching heat, and what an interesting corner of the world this was.

At one point she asked me why I wasn't working on television anymore. I pointed to our eleven-month-old daughter,

Ella, sleeping in my husband's arms. I related to her the path that had led me to that point and the events of the last year and a half of my life.

With tears in her eyes, she told me about her own daughter, just a couple of years younger than I. Her daughter had just had her first baby and was struggling with the adjustment to motherhood. "In her heart, she knows this is so important," the new grandmother explained. "But she is really struggling."

There are so many reasons why today's mothers struggle. Sheer exhaustion often tops the list. A lack of recognition for our efforts may also be included. But somewhere else on that list is this: many of us don't remember often enough that we are daughters of God, doing his work. An astute seven-year-old—a true princess in training—told her mom the other day, "Snow White is still pretty in rags." Indeed, we are all still daughters of God, no matter what we do, no matter where we labor. And when we place one woman ahead of another because of her calling or title, when riches are equated with business success and rags are equated with the "everydayness" of mothering, we are not only devaluing motherhood but belittling a daughter of God.

Devaluing motherhood devalues everything else women do. Consider this from Elder Bruce C. Hafen:

"We are losing what women have traditionally contributed

to cultural stability. Like the mortar that keeps a brick wall from toppling over, women have held together our most precious relationships: our marriages and child-parent ties. But now, we're seeing cracks in that mortar, which reveal some things we have too long taken for granted. . . .

"One woman's recent essay, 'Despising Our Mothers, Despising Ourselves,' reported that, despite many victories for women since the 1960s, the self-respect of American women is at an all-time low. Why? Because we've experienced not just a revolt against men's oppression but also a revolt against women: 'Heroic women who [dedicated] their lives to . . . children—as mothers, teachers, nurses, social workers—. . . [have been] made to feel stupid and second rate because they [took] seriously the Judeao-Christian precept that it was better to do for others than for oneself.' Devaluing motherhood devalues 'the primary work of most women throughout history,' which tells women they 'aren't worth serious consideration'" ("Women and the Moral Center of Gravity," in *Ye Shall Bear Record of Me*, 291, 293–94).

Is it any wonder, then, that we struggle as mothers to see our own worth? Satan has found a willing partner in the world to blind us and distract us with so many other "worthy endeavors" that we forget that motherhood is the most worthwhile venture of all.

Satan must love it when this happens, swooping down with

haste to sway our moods and tempt our souls! President Thomas S. Monson has said, "Occasionally discouragement may darken our pathway; frustration may be a constant companion. In our ears [we may hear] . . . Satan as he whispers, 'You cannot save the world; your small efforts are meaningless'" (in *Peace*, 50).

Like me, you've probably heard these whispers before. They are hard to avoid; and sometimes they aren't really whispers at all. Some in the world preach their version of success from megaphones on mountaintops. These voices bring fear, worry, discouragement, and numberless other negative feelings. They make motherhood seem like drudgery.

The *truth*—that motherhood is a noble, even heroic, occupation—is revealed in the same quiet but penetrating voice the Lord used to reveal his power to the Nephites. It was "not [in] a voice of thunder" but through a "still voice of perfect mildness, as if it had been a whisper, and it did pierce even to the very soul" (Helaman 5:30; see also 1 Kings 19:11–12).

Off to the Races

As our lives have become increasingly complicated—and loud—it has become more difficult to hear that "still voice of perfect mildness." And this is as Satan would have it. Sister Patricia Holland has said, "If I were Satan and wanted to destroy a society, I think I would stage a full-blown blitz on women. I would keep them so distraught and distracted that they would never find the calming strength and serenity for which their gender has always been known" (*On Earth As It Is in Heaven*, 85). This tactic seems to be working, doesn't it? Many times the still, small voice must compete with the frenzied cries that claim we can have everything—and have it all, now. Today's culture is very much about instant rewards, *measurables*, if you will, and immediate gratification.

"I increased sales by this much."

"I closed the deal."

"I won that case."

"Now, where's my reward?"

We want measurable, tangible results. We believe that doing something of worth means there are immediate rewards, that there is a garland of roses waiting for us at the end of the derby.

But motherhood is no horse race.

For one thing, motherhood lasts much longer than a two-minute ride. There are no celebratory songs, revelers on Millionaire's Row, or lovely hats to parade about in. Motherhood is often a solitary job, performed behind closed doors and within the solid walls of your own home. There is no one to cheer when you finally fold the last load of laundry for the day or get your sixteen-year-old to agree on an appropriate curfew. Because the world devalues the work a mother does (to say nothing of how hard that work is), motherhood is seldom given the respect it deserves. Even mothers themselves fall into this trap. Because it seems as though no one is watching or applauding, it is easy to forget how important our callings are.

Why? Because motherhood is all about selfless devotion, about doing "everyday things" every day. There are few instant rewards for mothers. Not a lot of immediate gratification, either. You don't gain political power or celebrity by being a mother. If anything, economically, you're set back by being a mother. Things are definitely more exciting—and more rewarding—at the races.

Or are they?

I'm willing to bet (no pun intended) that most of us don't remember what horse won the Kentucky Derby three years ago, or who owned the horse. On the other hand, I'm also willing to bet that your children can remember a trip to the park, a favorite family story, a late-night talk after a first date, and dozens of other things you have done each and every day as a mother.

President Joseph F. Smith said, "To do well those things which God ordained to be the common lot of all man-kind, is the truest greatness. To be a successful father or a successful mother is greater than to be a successful general or a successful statesman" (*Gospel Doctrine*, 285).

"A Purpose for Every Season"

As we listen to the words of the prophets of God—and believe them—we can get out of the horse race and find joy in the small, everyday events of life. Each woman who takes pride in her role as a mother teaches her children to value and respect motherhood. She will come to understand, through the still small voice, that "Motherhood is not what was left over after our Father blessed His sons with priesthood ordination. It was the *most ennobling endowment He could give His daughters*, a sacred trust that gave women an unparalleled role in helping His children keep their second estate" (Sheri Dew, "Are We Not All Mothers?" 96; emphasis added).

Let us learn to understand and live for the rich blessings that come with the "ennobling endowment" called motherhood.

Sisters, you are each in an amazing season of life. It is so important to understand that you don't have to do it all "right now," that there is a season for each of life's endeavors. I am convinced that when you use your time now—*when you live for the season you are in*—to love and teach your children, it cannot be misspent. Don't let the voices of the world distract you in your service. To paraphrase President James E. Faust, you need not sing all the verses of your song at the same time (see "A Message to My Granddaughters," 19).

A few years ago, I had the opportunity to interview Meg

Whitman at Princeton University. Meg is, of course, the CEO of eBay, with a net worth of a billion dollars. Meg was a lovely woman, gracious and kind. We had a wonderful conversation.

We talked about all sorts of things related to her many professional accomplishments. At one point, I asked her a question that I hadn't intended. And I was taken aback by her very honest reply.

"Looking back on it all," I said, "what's your biggest regret?"

Unlike her other responses, which had come quickly and easily, this answer came only after a thoughtful pause.

"Probably not spending as much time with the kids. . . . I did miss certain parts of their . . . development. I wasn't there to see some of the really fun things that they did. So I suppose the biggest regret is . . . it would be really great to have spent more time with them, particularly when they were little. . . . And you can't get that back."

She seemed willing to expound, and I continued, "So, the illusion that you can have it all . . . that it's out there . . . doesn't exist?"

"I actually don't think so. I think you can have a wonderful life, but you have to decide what trade-offs you're willing to make" (*The Early Show,* CBS, December 19, 2000).

To her words, I would add these: You must also decide that

mothers matter—that *you* matter. You are a daughter of God, doing His work.

One of my favorite quotes comes from C. S. Lewis and helps me remember that while I am in the process of building a firm foundation of love and righteousness for my children, the Lord is in the process of building me, his daughter. And knowing that God has a hand in my life makes everything I go through here— as a mother, a wife, and a woman—worthwhile:

"Imagine yourself as a living house. God comes in to rebuild that house. At first, perhaps, you can understand what He is doing. He is getting the drains right and stopping the leaks in the roof and so on: you knew that those jobs needed doing and so you are not surprised. But presently He starts knocking the house about in a way that hurts abominably and does not seem to make sense. What on earth is He up to? The explanation is that he is building quite a different house than the one you thought of—throwing out a new wing here, putting on an extra floor there, running up towers, making courtyards. You thought you were going to be made into a decent little cottage: but He is building a palace" (*Mere Christianity*, 205).

Maybe the next time someone asks, "What do you do?" you can say, with a twinkle in your eye, that you're a subcontractor, currently working on a palace or two.

chapter four

A MOTHER'S INFLUENCE

*Let France have good mothers,
and she will have good sons.*

—Napoleon Bonaparte

As a young correspondent at ABC News in 1996, I was assigned to cover Senator Bob Dole's presidential campaign. The experience involved a whirlwind of deadlines, long airplane rides, and very little sleep. The first time I climbed on board the campaign plane and saw dozens of veteran political correspondents typing on their laptops, talking a mile a minute on their cell phones, I knew I was in for a steep learning curve—and a lot of pressure.

Every night, my respite from a long day was a phone conversation with my mom. In whatever city, in whatever hotel—my mom got the lowdown on the day. Sometimes we'd talk for twenty seconds, sometimes twenty minutes. Nobody else in the world could possibly have been as interested as she was in how many cities we'd landed in that day or how many bad buffets I'd endured. She'd always finish the call with, "Is there anything I can do for you?" Always the answer: "I think I'm okay."

The most memorable part of the campaign was the last four days. Senator Dole had announced that he would crisscross the country, stopping in as many places as he could, sleeping only a couple of hours every night, all leading up to Election Day. I still have the red and white baseball cap his handlers passed out on the campaign bus: "96 Hours to a White House Beat." Well, it didn't quite work out that way, but the Senator gave it his best shot.

Twenty-four hours into that ninety-six-hour marathon I called my mom to tell her we would be passing through my hometown of Sacramento, California, the next day. I also mentioned, among a million other things, that my early morning live shots were getting pretty cold. It was an unseasonably chilly fall. "How could I have forgotten to bring a heavier coat?" I asked.

"You just didn't think you'd need it," she replied.

The next night we landed in Sacramento at the historic

railroad museum downtown. The Senator planned a 2 A.M. (yep, you read that right, 2 A.M.) rally with his supporters, and then we would be on to the next stop.

We arrived to a packed outdoor setup. Hundreds of Dole supporters were there, with big signs and lots of spirit. I made my way through the crowd and up to the platform where dozens of cameramen were setting up their shots. As I stood there looking over this huge crowd, two people caught my eye. For as long as I live I will never forget the image of my parents standing there, huddled together in the middle of a cold, northern California night.

My dad raised his hand to wave; my eyes lit up. And then I focused in on my mom. As always, she had a big, warm smile on her face. But this time she also had something else. There, folded over her arms, was my old green, wool, winter coat.

I worked my way through the throng of people to them, and we quickly exchanged hugs. Mom handed me the coat, and then I went on my way back through the crowd to prep for my live shot. Later, I found a note in the pocket: "I didn't want you to be cold *one more night.* Good luck. I love you!"

My coat provided so much more than physical warmth that chilly November night. Who else would have been so thoughtful? It was another reminder that my mom knew how to listen—how to really listen—and then how to act. That story is one of many I plan to tell my daughter, often. One I hope she'll tell her children, as well.

Do you ever wonder what stories your children will pass down about you?

A Legacy of Faithful Women

When Mark and I got married, we wrote down some goals for our family. At the top of the list was a desire to instill in our children a sense of family, a deep appreciation of their grandparents and great-grandparents and great-great-grandparents. We wanted them to be aware of their righteous heritage, one they will pass down to their own children.

So we turned our dining room into a family history room. The centerpiece of the room is a family tree that traces my mother's family back to the pioneers, to the *Mayflower*, and beyond. The tree itself is a family heirloom, hand-drawn by my great-grandfather. Displayed on the wall around that tree are photographs of our ancestors—grandparents, great-grandparents, and so on—great men and women who have carried our family names through the generations. The older the photograph, the better!

At family meals we pick a name off the tree or a photo from the wall and tell stories about that ancestor's life. We ask questions such as: What kind of person was she? What did he do?

What was she like? We read from journals and family histories and share memories that have been passed down over time.

We talk about Great-great-great Grandma Lorenda Thompson, who was one of the first pioneers to walk into the Salt Lake Valley in 1847. We remember Great-grandma Beulah Clayson, famous for her homemade, hand-dipped chocolates and her absolute devotion to the gospel. There is Great-great-grandmother Ellen Nilson, "Auntie Ella" as they called her, who had golden blonde hair that hung to the floor—and pages full of fascinating stories about her father who served as one of Brigham Young's bodyguards. We love to talk about Great-great-grandma Inger Elizabeth Anker, a marvelous cook and world-class donut maker, whose children remember her sweet treats but also recall passing by her room every night, where they'd find her quietly reading the Bible. Grandma Adriana Johnson studied opera at the New England Conservatory of Music and passed down a love of music to her descendants. There is also Great-grandmother Gladys Stratford, an elegant woman who loved beautiful hats and served as a faithful missionary in the Eastern States in the early 1930s. And Great-great-great-grandmother Malona Pratt, a gifted poetess and beloved daughter of an early apostle of the Church.

Each of these women has had a profound influence on our lives. I have learned that they found "nobility in motherhood and joy in womanhood" ("The Relief Society Declaration"). They nurtured, they loved, they persevered. I also imagine that they cleaned up a fair number of sticky messes and spent many long nights worrying and praying over their children and their children's choices. And, certainly, they provided warmth and love, twenty-four hours a day, seven days a week. I imagine that they, too, would have brought my coat to a crowded rally at two o'clock in the morning.

What Is a Mother's Influence?

Like my mother and her mother and all the others who came before me, my actions and choices will affect generations of mothers to come. Mothers are the single most powerful influence in a child's life, starting even before birth.

Author, obstetrician/gynecologist, and women's health expert Christiane Northrup, M.D., says, "Our mother provides us with our first experience of nurturing. She is our first and most powerful female role model. It is from her that we learn what it is to be a woman. . . . Our cells divided and grew to the beat of her heart. Our skin, hair, heart, lungs, and bones were nourished by her blood, blood that was awash with the neurochemicals formed in response to her thoughts, beliefs, and emotions. If she was fearful [or] anxious . . . , our bodies knew it. If she felt safe, happy, and fulfilled, we felt that too. . . .

"Every daughter contains her mother and all the women who came before her. The unrealized dreams of our maternal ancestors are part of our heritage" (*Mother-Daughter Wisdom*, 3).

But it is not only direct descendants who benefit from a mother's love and influence. Elder Bruce C. Hafen said, "Women have always lifted *entire cultures*. Their influence begins in each society's very core—the home. Here women have taught and modeled what social historian Alexis de Tocqueville called 'the habits of the heart,' the civilizing 'mores' or attitudes that create a sense of personal virtue and duty to the community, without which free societies can't exist" ("Women and the Moral Center of Gravity," in *Ye Shall Bear Record of Me*, 291–92).

How empowering! How true! It is mothers who teach future businessmen to be honest in their dealings. It is mothers who coach (and sometimes coax) future scientists, doctors, and mathematicians through worksheets and multiplication tables. It is mothers who show future politicians how to be compassionate—even in the face of opposition.

President Harold B. Lee taught that "a mother's heart is a child's schoolroom. The instructions received at the mother's knee . . . are never effaced entirely from the soul. . . . Family life is God's own method of training the young, and homes are largely what mothers make them" (*Teachings of Harold B. Lee*, 289).

President N. Eldon Tanner said, "A mother has far greater influence on her children than anyone else has, and she must realize that every word she speaks, every act, every response, her attitude, even her appearance and manner of dress, affect the lives of her children and the whole family. It is while the child is in the home that he gains from his mother the attitudes, hopes, and beliefs that will determine the kind of life he will live, and the contribution he will make to society" ("No Greater Honor: The Woman's Role," in *Woman*, 6–7).

Every word. Every act. Every response. Every attitude. That might make you want to pull the covers right back over your head! But it can also be comforting. When a mother teaches her child a truth, she adds a layer of insulation against Satan's influence—even as she struggles to hold that child's attention through a fifteen-minute family home evening lesson or insists that her little one says a simple bedside prayer.

Teaching Truth, Leaving Lasting Impressions

Author Ann Crittenden writes, "The more skillful the care-giver, the more invisible her efforts become. Ideally, the recipients themselves don't even notice that they are being cared for, other than to accept caring as part of the natural order of things. . . . Like the work of a fine seamstress, the *tiny stitches* that build character and confidence are *invisible to the eye*" (*The Price of Motherhood*, 72; emphasis added).

The stitches that build testimony and teach truth are also tiny, but they are often the very things that hold a soul together: family prayer, scripture study, family home evening, a shared testimony, a sympathetic hug, a smile. And it's the consistency of providing those things, day in and day out, that makes a difference and leaves a lasting impression.

We usually read Doctrine and Covenants 18:15 in the context of doing missionary work; but think how applicable the verse is to the work of mothers as well: "If it so be that you should labor all your days . . . and bring, save it be one soul unto me, how great shall be your joy."

"Laboring all your days" is difficult—often unseen—work, but its rewards are immeasurable. It would serve us well, as mothers, to remember this more often. It would also help to remember that there are many ways to "labor," each as appropriate as the other, and each necessary at different times and different stages of life. What really matters is that we labor with love and, as President Hinckley says, simply "do the very best [we] can" (*Teachings of Gordon B. Hinckley*, 392).

When I think of my own mother, I feel a profound sense of gratitude. She knew just what—and when—to do all the things a mother must. When we were little, she didn't worry so much about the dust and the dishes. Instead, she was down on the floor with us, playing in our pillow forts, or sitting at the piano helping us (or making us!) practice. She knew that there would be plenty of time later to scour the kitchen floor or polish the silver; but her children would be young for only a short while.

My mother was also quick to express love. Under my bed, I have a dozen shoe boxes filled with cards—cards for every occasion—all from my mom. Her notes always included little thoughts, quotes, and pick-me-ups. Sometimes they simply said, "I'm thinking about you!" Others carried reminders, "Remember to pray about that . . ." The first Christmas I was away from home as an adult, she made sure I had one present under my little twelve-inch tree, with a card that said: "I love you *always, always, always*. Love, Mom."

Years ago, I also watched my mother as she performed a service that no one else could.

I am the oldest of three children, with a sister, Hannah, and a brother, David. When David was just ten years old, he woke up one morning so sick he couldn't walk across the room. At first we all thought it was the flu. But a few days later, his condition had not improved. There were tests and trips to the doctor before learning that what we thought was the flu was really a brain tumor. David had cancer.

As the months passed, the trial unfolded . . . and the

treatments began. Radiation and chemotherapy are physically exhausting and emotionally draining for anyone, but perhaps especially challenging and cruel for a child.

Our family received so much support from friends and neighbors. Church members brought dinner to our house every night for months. And we all prayed—like never before. I dare say that no group of people had more faith than those who wished that David would be made strong and whole. I remember begging the Lord to give him strength, to make him well. That is what I wanted, and I know I wasn't alone.

After a few weeks, the treatments were over; but our little David was not healed. Bedridden, he could not speak, he could not smile, he could barely move. To communicate, our loving mother—whose prayers and tears and fears were greater than most of us could imagine—would sit by David's side and try to figure out exactly what he needed, what would make him most comfortable. She would go through the alphabet letter by letter. When the right letter came along, David would try to open his eyes. For hours, they would spell words this way, my mother quietly loving my brother—her son—and accepting the Lord's will. Day after day, I watched this . . . and I kept praying, *my* way.

Then, on one especially difficult night—when medication could barely dull the pain—my brother received a priesthood blessing. The blessing was short and ended with the words, "Thy will be done."

It takes a great deal of strength and faith to accept those four words, knowing *His* will may not be *your* will.

David passed away that night. He was just eleven years old.

I have missed him every day since. I have also often thought of the unspoken lessons my mother taught me about compassion, service, and pure Christ-like love—a mother's love.

President Spencer W. Kimball, in a letter read to the Church by his beloved Camilla, said, "No greater recognition can come to you in this world than to be known as a woman of God. No greater status can be conferred upon you than being a daughter of God who experiences true sisterhood, wifehood, and motherhood, or other tasks that influence lives for good" ("The Role of Righteous Women," 102).

My mother deserves this recognition.

My friend Whitney Johnson (I wish we were related!) also merits praise. She is a noble mother, who, not long ago, gathered her family together to create a "family mission statement."

Her nine-year-old son and five-year-old daughter helped compose it. It now stands as the centerpiece of their home, handwritten, on a piece of poster board and taped to the staircase by the front door. It reads:

Johnsons never give up.

Johnsons always tell the truth.

Johnsons support each other.

Johnsons testify of Jesus Christ in word and deed.

Johnsons fight against darkness.

Johnsons listen to the Spirit.

Johnsons have fun.

Johnsons are good friends, and

Johnsons stop eating when they are full!

What a wonderful reminder every day of the gospel principles that are surely practiced because of the noble mother in that home!

"Train up a child in the way he should go: and when he is old, he will not depart from it" (Proverbs 22:6).

Unafraid and Invincible

President Joseph F. Smith once said of Sister Eliza R. Snow: "She walked not on the borrowed light of others, but faced the morning unafraid and invincible" (as quoted in Ardeth G. Kapp, *My Neighbor, My Sister, My Friend*, 82). Sisters, you may not recognize it, but you, too, are unafraid and invincible. Even on the mornings when you're so tired you can barely butter your toast, the fact that you are up, willing to face the day and the challenges it holds, says everything about your courage and character.

It takes a lot of both to be a mother—and even greater faith to believe that you *can* make a difference. Your children are watching you. And they see the good you do. Even when it seems like they may not be listening, the truths you teach and represent are planting seeds of strength and faith in their minds and in their souls.

Not too many years ago, I was a junior in high school. I was seventeen years old and had been asked by a very nice and very handsome young man to go to the Senior Prom. I was *so* excited. The first thing I wanted to do was to go shopping for a dress, so my mom took me to the mall one Saturday to scout the stores.

Well, it took a while. Every dress we saw was either low cut . . . or no cut! Sleeveless, strapless, too short, slits up all sides.

Of course, all the dresses were considered "fashionable," and I told my mom over and over, "*All the other girls are wearing them, why can't I?*"

To this day, I can see my mother's face, and I can hear her speaking to me in a soft but sure voice: "Janie, you may not wear that. It is not modest. It is not appropriate."

Well, I nagged and I complained. I did all those things teenage girls do. I told her it wasn't fair, that she was surely going to ruin my life! I didn't make it easy for her, but she held firm. In the gospel of Jesus Christ, modesty is always in fashion. The prophets have told us that our standards are not socially negotiable, and my mother believed that.

After a long day of searching, we finally bought a beautiful, long pink taffeta dress. It was the most modest one we could find—and yet it still wasn't quite ready to wear. So my mom took it to a seamstress and had some extra material put over the shoulders to make it pretty and suitable for my high school dance.

The senior prom came and went. We had a great time. And sure enough, most of my girlfriends showed up wearing those low-cut dresses my mom and I had seen in the stores.

The next day, the phone rang. It was my date's father, who also happened to be a counselor in our stake presidency. President Smith was calling to thank my mother for dressing me like a Latter-day Saint young woman *should* be dressed.

My mother was and is a mother of nobility. She never wavered in her standards or her expectations of me, whether it was regarding my clothing or my curfew or spiritual matters. How grateful I am now that she held strong.

For when that day comes—and it will come—when my own daughter will say, "Well, all the other girls are wearing it," or, "All the other girls are doing it, why can't I?"—it will help me to have the courage to say, as my mother did to me: "You may not wear that. It is not modest. It is not appropriate."

Now, fast forward with me to a day fifteen years after that prom date.

I was in New York City, anchoring *The Early Show,* when I was asked to do a photo shoot for a popular women's magazine. I arrived at the water-front studio overlooking the Statue of Liberty to find an elaborate setup. There were more than a dozen people setting up the shoot—set decorators, lighting experts, hair and makeup artists, stylists, caterers. It was clear that a lot of time and money had been spent in preparation for this event.

After a few minutes of settling in, I was taken to a dressing room where a rack of clothes had been gathered for me to wear on camera. As I examined the outfits, I became more and more uncomfortable. They were designer clothes. More than thirty outfits. Expensive fashions you'd find in the chic-est boutiques in New York.

There was only one problem: I couldn't wear any of them.

It seems not much had changed since my days in high school. Everything was either low cut . . . or no cut. Sleeveless, strapless, too short, slits up all sides.

As I sat in that dressing room wondering what I was going to do, I said a prayer and asked Heavenly Father to help me. Almost immediately, the words of my mother came to my mind from those many years before: "Janie, you may not wear that. It is not modest. It is not appropriate."

I could feel her strength, and I remembered how she didn't back down, as difficult as it was—and as uncomfortable as I made her feel.

I knew what I needed to do.

Needless to say, the magazine editor was not at all happy when I told her I couldn't wear the clothes she'd selected for me. She said things like, "What's the problem?" "These are the latest styles." "This is what women are wearing!"

I just calmly said, over and over, "I'm sorry, I can't wear them."

She stomped off, and I thought for sure the shoot was over.

I was collecting my bags to leave when this editor caught me at the door. "We're gathering new clothes for you," she said. "They should be here within a half hour."

As I think of my mother and all the mothers out there who wonder if they can really make a difference, President Kimball's words speak to my heart: "To be a righteous woman is a glorious thing in any age. To be a righteous woman during the winding-up scenes on this earth, before the second coming of our Savior, is an especially noble calling. The righteous woman's strength and influence today can be tenfold what it might be in more tranquil times" (*My Beloved Sisters*, 17).

To my mother, my grandmothers, my great-grandmothers, and all the women who make a difference—who are unafraid and invincible in the everyday challenges of mothering—I dedicate this chapter to you.

chapter five

CAN I QUIT NOW?

❧

You can't possibly do this alone, but you do have help.
The Master of Heaven and Earth is there to bless you. . . .
Rely on Him. Rely on Him heavily. Rely on Him forever.

—Jeffrey R. Holland, "Because She Is a Mother," 37

After our son William was born prematurely, he spent eleven long weeks in the Neonatal Intensive Care Unit (NICU). I was so frightened for him. He was very sick. And so was I.

My caesarean section had a lot of complications, including a bad infection, and I was in tremendous pain for several weeks. It seemed as if every minute was full of stress—and sorrow. Getting up throughout the night to pump breast milk, driving about an hour roundtrip to the hospital every day to deliver my milk and visit little William, taking care of fifteen-month-old Ella—who was really still a baby herself. There were so many days I remember feeling as though I couldn't go on, I just couldn't do it one more minute.

During this time, my husband was my rock—always strong, always prayerful, always optimistic. Some nights he would come home to find me curled up into a ball on the couch, barely functioning. So often, he would gently, quietly place his hands on my head and, with great faith, draw on the powers of heaven as he administered beautiful priesthood blessings. There were moments I could actually feel an indescribable warmth flowing from his hands into my head and then passing through my body. I had never experienced anything like it.

During this time, so many people said to us, "We've been praying for you. We've been praying for William." I also had never felt so buoyed up by the power of prayer.

Indeed, it seemed that each time I said a prayer to ask Heavenly Father to help me, to get me through a particular moment, He would send an angel—in the form of some person—to help me.

Every day, a wonderful woman from our ward would come to our home to take care of Ella while I traveled to and from the hospital. One friend worked with my visiting teachers to prepare a rotation schedule; and for the better part of two months women volunteered to help us. Like clockwork, every morning, somebody would show up on my doorstep, ready for duty!

Not only did they care for my daughter while I was away; but I would come home every day to discover extraordinary acts of kindness: baskets of laundry washed and folded, a pot roast in the oven for dinner, my kitchen scrubbed spotless.

My dear sister, Hannah, who was a new mother herself and a new Relief Society president put her life on hold and brought her own little baby to Boston to help our family. She researched books about premature birth and ordered special preemie hospital outfits online. And during her first visit to the NICU, she quietly began measuring the Isolette, then hand-sewed two beautiful blankets to fit over the top of the incubator.

An old friend in Colorado sent me a card from her next-door neighbor, who was a total stranger to me but had heard about our situation and wanted me to know she, too, had had a baby born at twenty-seven weeks' gestation—just like William. Taped inside her note was a photo of her daughter, now seven years old. She wanted me to know that there was hope and light at the end of my tunnel. She included this poem, which I literally carried around with me during that whole time—and which I still keep in my kitchen to read every day:

DON'T QUIT

When things go wrong, as they sometimes will,

When the road you're trudging seems all up hill,

When the funds are low and the debts are high,

And you want to smile, but you have to sigh,

When care is pressing you down a bit,

Rest if you must, but don't you quit. . . .

Success is failure turned inside out.

The silver tint of the clouds of doubt,

And you never can tell how close you are,

It may be near when it seems so far,

So stick to the fight when you're hardest hit.

It's when things seem worst that you must not quit.

—Author Unknown

Well, I didn't quit, and neither did William or Ella or my sweet husband. We were finally able to bring William home from the hospital, and life moved forward.

Many months passed and William was healthy now—a bright and happy little baby. But boxes of Cheerios were still being dumped out on the floor, we still had meltdowns near naptime, I still had to wake up every three hours through the night, and I still caught myself wondering if I was really up to this—how could I be a successful mother, teacher, and guide to these precious children whom God had entrusted to me?

The poet William Ross Wallace wrote that "The hand that rocks the cradle is the hand that rules the world." I love those words. I even believe them; but how can I rule the world when I can't keep my eyes open?

Can I Really Do This?

Motherhood is tough work, and there are days when giving two weeks' notice seems to be the best way—the only way—to escape the chaos.

Before I was a mother, the job didn't appear to be that difficult. *How hard can it be?* I thought. I'd traveled around the world, worked twenty-hour days for days on end, met tough deadlines, parried with the smartest of people. I was certain I could do *mothering.*

Then Ella was born three weeks early, by C-section, and I felt like I'd been hit with a brick. I remember walking downstairs one morning, still rubbing the sleep out of my eyes, to find my mother in the kitchen. There she was, with the baby in one arm, and somehow managing—simultaneously—the scrambled eggs on the stove, a batch of banana bread on the counter, a pile of folded laundry on the couch, and a phone conversation. I burst out crying, thinking over and over again, *I'll never be able to do this!*

My friend Sara often refers to mothering as "The Ironman [Competition] of Living." Exactly! We go into motherhood expecting that it will require some strength; then we find ourselves in it and realize we're completely out of breath—with miles left to go. Indeed, motherhood is an extraordinary test of endurance and strength, some days requiring that we sprint, and other days asking us to swim uphill against the current.

And somehow, no one seems to mention this to women before the babies come!

The Myths

The shelves at my local bookstore are full of books on mothering and parenthood. There is truly an expert answer—somewhere—for every child-rearing question a mom, of any age, can think of: How do I get my newborn to latch on? How do I get my two-year-old to sleep through the night? How do I get my five-year-old to listen? Should my eleven-year-old really be watching this much TV? Is it safe for my fifteen-year-old to frequent that Internet chat room? How will my grandchildren wade through all that is unclean and harmful in this world? Each question has its own answer—all wrapped up in a box and tied with a pretty bow. The experts likely have good intentions. But I've found that many mothers, after sifting through all the answers, feel worse because they feel inadequate; for so much of the advice fails to address their real concerns—*Is it supposed to be this hard? No one told me it would be like this—am I doing something wrong? Will my children turn out okay, despite my inadequacies?*

Just before Ella was born, my friend Elayne, a lawyer, sent me a letter in which she said: "I wish I had known, when I had my daughter nine years ago, exactly what this adventure entailed. But to be honest, I was pretty clueless about how to be a mother. I felt overwhelmed and really stressed the first six months or so. It was such a huge change from my previous life."

For some reason, most women enter motherhood expecting quiet days of rocking babies, singing lullabies, and visiting their local library for story time. And, though there *are* quiet days and happy songs and great stories that will unfold for years and years of mothering, most mothers aren't quite prepared for just how hard this work really is. Wouldn't it be helpful to have a handbook that lists all the "myths of mothering?" Here are some I'd like to debunk:

Myth 1: You will be in control . . . you are the mother, after all! One morning, before I became a mother, I was just about to walk out the door for work when the phone rang. It was the executive producer of *48 Hours*, who was calling with some big news: Jessica Lynch—a U.S. soldier who had been captured in Iraq—had been found alive at a hospital in Baghdad.

This producer wanted me to travel to Jessica's small hometown outside Charleston, West Virginia, to try to get an interview with her family. "There's a 9:30 flight out of LaGuardia," she said. "We'll take care of the ticket . . . just go to the airport, show your ID, and your reservation will be there."

I scrambled to throw a few outfits in a bag then raced outside to hail a cab. I got to the airport, got my E-ticket out of the machine, literally ran to the gate, and squeaked onto that plane just before the cabin door was shut. It was a fairly uneventful flight. I did some reading on the plane—research faxed to me at home, about Jessica, her military unit, and what little anybody knew about her family.

We finally landed in Charleston. I got off the plane and rushed out past security to find Charlie, an associate producer who was already on the ground and was supposed to meet me. I got to the baggage claim and looked around . . . I didn't see anybody I knew.

No problem, I thought, *happens all the time. I'll just call him and arrange a meeting location.*

We arranged to meet at the Avis rental car counter, where I arrived within minutes. Two, three, five minutes passed, and there was still no sign of Charlie. It was quite unlike him to be late or not follow through, so I called him again.

"I'm here," I said.

"Well, I'm here, too."

"At Avis?"

"Yup, right in front of the big red sign."

"Me, too."

"Are you sure there's not more than one Avis counter?"

The agent at the Avis desk confirmed that this was, indeed, the one and only Avis counter in the airport.

I thought I was losing my mind. *What was going on?*

As I turned around in circles, scanning everything around me for a clue as to what could possibly be happening, my eye caught sight of a young woman sitting on a bench just a few feet from me.

She had three little children—a toddler and twin babies. All three of them were restless and crying as she tried to calm them and meet their needs. I seemed to be an amusing diversion for her as she watched and listened to my situation unfolding.

Finally, she looked at me and smiled. Then, somewhat embarrassed for me but feeling she needed to help, she said, "Honey, I didn't think it was possible, but you're having a worse day than I am! You're in Charleston, *South Carolina*. Not Charleston, *West Virginia!*"

Now that I have two babies of my own, and a few long airplane rides under our belts, I sometimes wonder if she was really right!

One of the hardest lessons in mothering is learning to recognize that you are no longer in control. How many times have you started out the day hoping to move one direction, or to arrive at a particular destination, or accomplish just one task, only to make it to the end of the day and discover that you're in the wrong place altogether, miles from where you hoped to be?

I eventually did make it to the right Charleston—albeit after midnight—and got the interviews I needed. Looking back now, that moment in the airport is laugh-out-loud funny. But at the time, it was all I could do not to throw my arms up in the air and call it a day.

Motherhood is much the same way. It's all about seeing the big picture, especially when so many things you do don't last— folded laundry, washed dishes, a clean house. We simply cannot control another individual's temperament or behavior. But we can use those moments when we want to throw in the towel to our advantage.

So many times, the mundane tasks—or the "Surprise! You must now mop up an entire carton of milk off your newly washed floor" or the "I'm sorry, Mom, I had no idea it was 1:00 A.M. *already*" moments—provide extraordinary teaching opportunities. If you can control *your* behavior when everything around you is out of control, you can model for your children a valuable lesson in patience and understanding . . . and snatch an opportunity to shape character.

This is what the Lord would want us to do, to look beyond today to eternity, to truly look at our children and do our best to teach them well—even if we can't always control what they do.

Myth 2: Needing help is a sign of weakness. When William was in the NICU and the women in my ward united to help me take care of my little family, I learned, among so many other things, that I was not alone. I had a "family" of sisters who would help me get through this. In truth, every woman in the Church should feel she is a member of this same family. Because that means that you *don't* have to be alone as you make your way through motherhood. It's *okay* to ask for help.

In fact, some of the best friendships are developed between mothers who are willing to empathize when sorrow sets in, to listen when you simply need someone to talk to, or to pitch in when things get tough.

Not too long ago, during a trip to Salt Lake City, I was asked to be a guest on a morning TV program at one of the local stations. "Bring the kids," the producer said. "We'd like to have them on for a few minutes." Before the show, I packed our little ones in the car to run to the market for some diapers. I planned to grab the diapers then head back to my friend Susan's house, where we were staying, to pick up some papers before we rushed into town for our little appearance.

We were in the car when the morning took an unexpected turn.

Even though he'd eaten just about an hour before, William started crying in a sudden burst of hunger . . . and, as luck would have it, I had forgotten his bottle. I sped up a bit to try to hurry home. But in my focused attempt to calm one child, I noticed that Ella had become very quiet and quite pale. Within a few minutes we'd pulled into Susan's driveway, with William still wailing in his seat.

I quickly pulled the baby out of the car and rushed to Ella's side to let her out, too. As I leaned in, Ella suddenly unloaded her breakfast (and what looked like most of her last *three* meals!) all over her car seat, all over herself, and all over me. It was everywhere—in my hair, on my clothes—a huge, gross mess.

We walked into Susan's house through the garage: one *screaming* baby, one *carsick* baby, and one *totally overwhelmed* mother. At that moment, all I wanted to do was go back to bed.

Susan met me in the hallway. I don't know how she didn't burst out laughing. All I could say, so pathetically, was "Can you help me?"

"Oh my goodness!" she said. "Let me take the baby."

I quickly ran upstairs with Ella and cleaned and changed us both. Then I ran back out to the car, ready to clean up round two—and try to make our appointment.

Too late for cleanup. There was Susan—busy getting her own three kids off to school and already late for her own hectic workday—there she was . . . with my baby in one arm, sponge and towels in hand, already cleaning up the mess.

A little piece of me was embarrassed, horrified actually, that my dear friend had cleaned my toddler's sickening mess. A bigger piece of me was so grateful.

Author Anna Quindlen says, "The great motherhood friendships are the ones in which two women can admit [how difficult mothering is] quietly to each other, over cups of [herbal] tea at a table sticky with spilled apple juice and littered with markers without tops" (*Loud and Clear,* 30).

If you *let* yourself *ask* for help, and allow yourself to graciously accept it, you may receive more than just a lift or a moment of peace—you may form a deep connection—you may find a friend.

It's also important to remember that our greatest friend and ally is the Savior. At a recent General Relief Society Meeting, President Gordon B. Hinckley told this story:

"Some years ago in the Salt Lake Tabernacle, Elder Marion D. Hanks conducted a panel discussion. Included in that panel was an attractive and able young woman, divorced, the mother of seven children then ranging in ages from 7 to 16. She said that one evening she went across the street to deliver something to a neighbor. Listen to her words, as I recall them:

"'As I turned around to walk back home, I could see my house lighted up. I could hear echoes of my children as I had walked out of the door a few minutes earlier. They were saying: "Mom, what are we going to have for dinner?" "Can you take me to the library?" "I have to get some poster paper tonight." Tired and weary, I looked at that house and saw the light on in each of the rooms. I thought of all of those children who were home waiting for me to come and meet their needs. My burdens felt heavier than I could bear.

" 'I remember looking through tears toward the sky, and I said, "Dear Father, I just can't do it tonight. I'm too tired. I can't face it. I can't go home and take care of all those children alone. Could I just come to You and stay with You for just one night? I'll come back in the morning."

" 'I didn't really hear the words of reply, but I heard them in my mind. The answer was: "No, little one, you can't come to me now. You would never wish to come back. But I can come to you" ' " ("In the Arms of His Love," 117).

Myth 3: You must do it all, all the time. Sometime in the last thirty years or so, someone invented the term *supermom.*

Much like Superman—who possesses extraordinary strength and X-ray vision—a supermom is a woman who can do it all: laundry, housework, child rearing, yard care, carpools, music lessons, scrapbooking, soccer practice, art projects, homework, career work, PTA work, church work, family work, and on and on and on. Sounds pretty great, right? And completely exhausting and never-ending and lonely, even.

Sometimes—most times—you *can't* do it all. And that's okay.

My friend Lisa is a firm believer in time-outs; not for her children—for herself! When all of the kids are ornery and pressures are mounting and Lisa thinks she just might blow her top, she heads for time-out. Usually, time-out is in the bathroom, where she locks the door, has a good cry, says a quick prayer, or just takes some time to breathe deeply before facing reality again.

If there's one thing I'm trying to learn, it is this: We need to give ourselves permission to take a break . . . and more than a couple of minutes resting on the bathroom floor.

I often still recall the words of William's very wise primary care nurse in the NICU. She was one of the most veteran nurses in the unit, smart and very experienced. One day I must have looked particularly wiped out. Pat pulled up a rocker next to me, then pulled out a big plastic bowl of homemade chicken noodle soup.

"I made this for you last night," she said, smiling. "When I need to do something good for myself, I make this soup."

I could smell it. It smelled simply delicious. So delicious that I could almost feel the nutrients seeping into me through my nose!

Pat then placed one hand on William's head and one hand on my shoulder and said with some concern, "You need to give yourself *permission* to take a break. If you don't take care of yourself, you can't take care of your baby."

She was right.

Our dear prophet, President Gordon B. Hinckley, has said as much: "Our lives become extremely busy. We run from one thing to another. . . . We are entitled to spend some time with ourselves in introspection, in development" ("Life's Obligations," 5).

Centuries ago, even the great prophet Moses needed reminding that he couldn't do it all. Moses was daily sitting before the people, hearing all their concerns and squabbles, trying to provide answers to all of their questions, when his father-in-law, Jethro, asked, "What is this thing that thou doest to the people? why sittest thou thyself alone, and all the people stand by thee from morning unto even?" (Exodus 18:14).

Moses explained what he was trying to do—serve as sole judge of the Israelites—and his wise father-in-law replied: "The thing that thou doest is not good. Thou wilt surely wear away, both thou, and this people that is with thee: for this thing is too heavy for thee; thou art not able to perform it thyself alone" (vv. 17–18).

As a mother, what sorts of things are you doing that "wilt surely wear [you] away"?

Moses was counseled to solicit help from others and to let them bear the burden with him. He was promised that "if thou shalt do this thing, and God command thee so, then thou shalt be able to endure" (v. 23).

This promise can be true for us as well. When we take time to refocus ourselves, to center ourselves, to take care of ourselves, to allow others to help us, we can more easily remember what is important—we can endure.

God counseled Moses to look at the big picture, to let go of the little issues that could be worked out on their own.

Likewise, I believe that God is more concerned with the "big picture" in our lives, more concerned that we love our children and less concerned that we provide them with two or three music lessons; more concerned that we spend time with them and less concerned about how many hours we volunteer with the PTA; more concerned that we talk with our teenagers and less concerned that we finish the laundry.

Don't waste your time trying to do it all! If you do, you may miss the best parts. Motherhood is the ideal time to "live in the moment" because it is the perfect time to see life in action, to witness your child taking his first step, picking her first flower, walking out the door for his first day of school, or leaving with a fine young man on her first date. These things will never happen again.

I love this oft-quoted proverb, which seems so applicable to my life right now:

> *Cleaning and scrubbing can wait for tomorrow,*
> *For babies grow up, I've learned, to my sorrow.*
> *So quiet down, cobwebs. Dust, go to sleep.*
> *I'm rocking my baby, and babies don't keep.*
>
> —Author unknown

Teenagers grow up fast, too. And so do grandchildren. Wouldn't it be great if we could somehow just slow down and really watch our children—at every age—change before our eyes?

Rather than trying to be Supermom, try being simply Mom— and let the wonder in your child's eyes give you the strength to keep on going.

Myth 4: Motherhood means a loss of identity. One of Satan's most clever traps of late has been to convince women that once they become mothers they are no longer the women they used to be, that they've lost themselves.

Certainly, motherhood involves some sacrifices. Every worthwhile venture does. You will certainly lose some sleep over the years, and, every now and then, you might temporarily lose your sanity. But you will also learn—about yourself, about the world, about the Spirit. The woman you can become as you nurture your children is a woman of faith, a woman who trusts in the Lord and knows he has a plan for her, a woman who has developed patience and empathy and knows how to listen, a woman of courage.

As you learn these things, and as you grow into the woman *God knows you can be,* inevitably little pieces of you will rub off on your children—and their children. And on it goes . . .

You do not lose your identity when you become a mother; you have the opportunity to more closely *identify with God,* to become more like Him and to enrich the lives of all who come after you.

I am both a mother and a stepmother. Before my husband joined the Church, he was divorced. So my first encounters with motherhood were not with newborn Ella, but with Mark's three children.

At first, I was completely overwhelmed by the idea of being a mother to three children who were not "my own." I remember when Mark and I were dating and we had been talking about getting married. One night we were driving in the car and I said, quite bluntly, "I can't marry you. I'll never be able to take care of your children."

On top of that, having stepchildren was not in my "plan"—it was not the picture I had painted for myself. It's just not what I had envisioned. *What will people say,* I thought. *What will the Christmas card look like?* (Imagine that!?!)

Of course, Heavenly Father didn't have those same concerns. After some prayer and reflection on my part, I felt a strong, very specific prompting: *These children will bring you joy.*

Just a few weeks later, Mark and I got engaged. On the night we told the kids we were going to be married, I made dinner . . . and Mark made the announcement. The two younger kids started screaming "Hurray, Hurray!" Twelve-year-old Kristina started crying.

I was worried. This can't be good!

I'll never forget what she said, in a really sweet, soft voice: "I'm so happy. I'm so happy for you . . . and I'm so happy for me."

Kristina, Mark, and Kathryn *have* brought me incredible joy. They have been respectful and wonderful. I love it when they come to stay with us every other weekend. They fill our house with laughter and excitement (lots of laundry and messes, too!).

They play with Ella and William and protect them and love them.

Still, it can be difficult, and sometimes, even now, I resist it.

For example, my first freelance work after Ella was born was a two-day project, hosting a program on the Discovery Health Network. It was my first paycheck in a while, and I was actually excited to think that maybe I could take just a little bit of that money and splurge on something fun. We needed a new couch, among other things.

But since Mark and I had been married and moved into a new home and had two children, there weren't enough beds, or bedrooms, to hold our growing family. I got the real feeling that when Mark's children came to visit that they felt crowded out— they didn't feel completely comfortable or fully incorporated into our home . . . simply because there wasn't enough room.

So, I remember one night, again, happily saying my prayers, when the thought came to me that we needed to use my small paycheck to help turn our attic into a bedroom and refinish the old bathroom up there for the kids.

Long story short: I didn't want to do it. I didn't want to sacrifice part of myself for three little people. I didn't want to use that money to renovate a room we didn't "need" and that I personally would not use. The funds would be better used elsewhere. Period.

But the prompting didn't go away. It kept coming back. And as I wrestled with my emotions, I started thinking: *Am I going to welcome these children into my life—or not? Am I going to accommodate them and their needs—or not? Am I going to show them that I love them—or not?*

Slowly I began to really feel that this *was* the best thing for our family; it was the best thing for "our" children.

So we took that money and hired a friend to redo the attic.

Well, the kids *love* it. They have a place to go, a place to sleep that's all their own, when they come to our house. Although I resisted at first, it makes me so happy now to know they are happy. And it showed me that there is still so much more that Heavenly Father wants to teach me, so much more he believes I can become.

And rather than *losing* my identity with the children, the irony is, I actually feel as though I have further identified my *true self*. I've worked my way through often difficult and complicated, but very human, emotions . . . and found love and peace and tremendous happiness.

Revelations

Debunking these myths over the last few years has been enlightening.

But even more enlightening are the real answers, the

revelations and miracles we, as mothers, are entitled to. When Mark and I were sealed in the Salt Lake Temple, the sealer gave me—as a woman—some very powerful counsel. It pertains to all of us, as women in this gospel. He said: "Sometimes in the Church we tend to think of the men as the scholars—and the women as the compassionate servants. We must change that.

"Jane," he said, "you should be able to teach the Atonement as deeply and as insightfully as your husband.

"And Mark," he said, "Jane can cook the casserole . . . but you can deliver it!"

I sometimes think we underestimate the unique privilege and responsibility it is to bear and nurture children, the power we have to teach—and to be taught—by the Spirit.

It is not only in her calling as a Young Women president, or a Primary teacher, or a visiting teacher, that a woman can be magnified. You can be magnified in your calling as a mother. You must simply ask for the Spirit to guide you.

Women who pray in faith receive revelation, particularly as it relates to the nurture and rearing of children. And the more we act on revelation, the more we are able to receive.

I love reading about Rebekah, who waited twenty long years to bear a child. During her pregnancy, she felt the children within her womb struggling. Rebekah and Isaac had entreated the Lord for the blessing of having children; and Rebekah likely wondered how the Lord could bless her with the desire of her heart but still allow this struggle within her. "If it be so," she asked, "why am I thus? And she went to enquire of the Lord" (Genesis 25:22). In other words, she was uncomfortable, possibly worried about the children she was carrying, and, like mothers all over the world today, she went to the Lord in prayer. He answered, revealing to her the future of her lineage: "Two nations are in thy womb, and two manner of people shall be separated from thy bowels; and the one people shall be stronger than the other people; and the elder shall serve the younger" (Genesis 25:23).

Elder Bruce R. McConkie said this: "May I now take our common ancestor, Rebekah, as a pattern for what her daughters in the Church today can do? She did not say, 'Isaac, will you inquire of the Lord. You are the patriarch; you are the head of the house,' which he was. She went to inquire of the Lord, and she gained the answer.

"When Rebekah was troubled and needed divine guidance she herself took the matter up with the Lord, and he spoke to her in reply. The Lord gives revelation to women who pray to him in faith" (as cited in *Old Testament Gospel Doctrine Teacher's Manual*, 45). The spirit of revelation has the power to soothe, the power to guide, and the power to make everyday mothering something women want to embrace, something they will help each other through.

It will still be hard—anything that is worthwhile is usually difficult. But I testify that it *is* possible "to be a joyful mother of children" (Psalm 113:9).

We have the Lord to help us.

And, sometimes, we have our children to encourage us.

In our house, through the pure heart and robust vocal cords of a two-year-old, we feel a lot of encouragement. And it seems that we often shout for joy.

Our little Ella loves "the happy song" from the *Children's Songbook* ("If You're Happy," 266). Every day, many, many times a day, Ella will say to me, "Happy song, Mama, happy song!" And whether we're in the grocery store or at the bank or in the bathtub, we'll sing the song, throw our arms up in the air, and shout "Hurray!"

And I will smile.

And, in that moment, feel joy.

chapter six

WALKING IN EACH OTHER'S SHOES

It is not for you to be led by the women of the world; it is for
you to lead the . . . women of the world, in everything that
is praise-worthy, everything that is God-like, everything
that is uplifting and that is purifying to the children of men.

—Joseph F. Smith, *Teachings of Joseph F. Smith*, 184

During my years as a journalist I conducted a lot of celebrity interviews, some more memorable than others. A few transcended the standard question-and-answer session. One of the latter was in the Los Angeles home of comedienne Phyllis Diller. I was hosting a television special on Bob Hope and had asked Phyllis to give us her unique perspective on the legendary actor and comedian. Phyllis had spent many years traveling and performing with Bob Hope on USO tours. I was told she even had a "Bob Hope room" in her house, complete with a huge picture of him hanging on the wall.

Phyllis, of course, was a character herself. Considered a pioneer of female stand-up comedy, she was famous for her outlandish wigs and quick wit. Before I arrived at her door, I had done my homework—read some articles, watched several clips. The Phyllis I researched seemed loud, irreverent, kind of crazy, and, to be frank, a bit grating—what with that wild hair and cackling laugh.

When I arrived with my crew, Phyllis welcomed us into her living room for our conversation. She showed us walls and walls hung with memorabilia from decades in Hollywood. We must have chatted for more than an hour before we finally rolled tape. Sitting to the side of her big, black, grand piano I asked my first question. "Do you remember the first time you met Bob Hope?"

She started to answer, "Ohhh, yes—"

Then she stopped. In classic Phyllis Diller form she let out a huge roar of a laugh and looked down—at my feet. Yes, my feet.

"I'm sorry, dear, but before we begin, I have to ask you: what size shoe do you wear?"

I started to laugh myself. "7½ AA."

"That's what I thought," she said, ripping the microphone off her lapel. "We wear the same size!"

Phyllis grabbed my hand, pulled me out of my chair, and started to lead me out of the room. My producer and camera crew were wondering what in the world was going on. So was I!

We landed, of all places, in her closet—which was about the size of my living room. There were stacks of hats up to the ceiling, gowns of every style—from every era—and rows and rows of shoes. There must have been 200 pairs. I found myself spinning around trying to take it all in. My eyes finally landed on Phyllis, who was down on her knees, carefully and methodically emptying the racks until a heap of shoes appeared in the middle of the closet floor. After a couple of minutes, she stopped. And in a tone and expression I hadn't yet heard from her during our visit, she said quietly, "Sit down, would you? I've been waiting for someone who would listen to the stories of my shoes."

Indeed, every shoe had a story.

The custom-made Italian shoes had carried her across the stage to banter with Bob Hope and entertain our troops during the height of the Vietnam War. She loved the hot pink pumps she wore as the mystery guest on the popular TV show *What's My Line.* There were the flat brown sandals that took her on humanitarian trips to help poor children around the world. Phyllis was a painter and a concert pianist, and she wore sleek, black-sequined sling-backs as a soloist with a symphony orchestra. Some of the shoes reminded her of occasions with her children . . . she'd raised five. And she was a grandmother several times over.

With each story, we'd try on a shoe. We sat in that closet for almost an hour. And with every story, my impressions of Phyllis changed. The image I'd created in my mind hadn't painted a complete picture. I began to appreciate her many extraordinary talents. She'd had a lot of excitement—that was obvious. But she'd struggled, too; and that's what most people didn't see. There were health problems. She'd lost a husband. She'd struggled to help a daughter with schizophrenia. Her life was not all laughs.

When Phyllis finished her final story, we were back to work.

By the end of our visit I had found a friend.

A few days passed, and I was home in New York when there came a knock at my apartment door. It was a deliveryman, who handed me a big, black, hard-backed suitcase. As I opened it, I smiled. *Shoes* began to topple out . . . at least twenty-five pairs of Phyllis Diller's favorites!

All these years later, I treasure that black suitcase. Our daughter Ella loves to play dress-up in Phyllis's shoes now. If she only knew!

Someday I will tell her about the lesson I learned from my

encounter with Phyllis Diller. How I had walked into the home of the "crazy lady with the wild hair," but as I stood in her shoes, literally and figuratively, I began to see a completely different person—someone warm, kind, vulnerable.

A Day in Another Mother's Shoes

I think we too often categorize others, labeling them without really knowing them. We look at wild hair or a crazy laugh or unkempt children or a messy house and make hasty judgments.

The saying "Don't judge someone until you've walked a mile in her shoes" never seemed more true than it did that day in Phyllis Diller's closet . . . until I became a mother and quickly discovered how vital it is to stop judging and start loving.

My friend Anne is a bright, accomplished, righteous woman. I feel happy and uplifted when she is around. Her heart is so pure.

Anne's husband is also a wonderful man, kind and good.

But for years he lived with a debilitating illness, which made it difficult for him to work. It affected everything in his life, including his ability and desire to attend church.

With no income and with debt piling up, the family was struggling . . . emotionally, spiritually, and financially. And Anne realized that she was going to have to support her children. So, after much fasting and prayer, she took a job. Her husband, with ongoing help from family and friends, would stay home and do what he could to take care of their kids. There was really no other choice. Anne had come to terms with the fact that this was the way it had to be, at least for a while. Things were difficult. Anne had never expected this; but she was willing to do whatever the Lord asked on behalf of her family.

One Sunday, in the midst of this difficult period, Anne was sitting in Relief Society, waiting for the meeting to begin. The woman next to her began asking Anne how her husband was doing and how things were going at home.

Anne hadn't talked much about her circumstance, but she decided to confide in this sister. "Things are stable," Anne told her. "I've started working. My husband is staying home with our children."

The look on this woman's face said as much as the words that came out of her mouth. "Oh," she said. "So, how do you reconcile that with the Proclamation on the Family?"

Anne was devastated. She told me later how difficult it was that at precisely the moment when, more than anything else, all she needed was love and support, she had been judged instead.

"If *she* feels that way," Anne told me, "*everybody* must feel that way."

And so Anne felt more and more isolated . . . and very much alone.

If *only* that sister had been able to stand in Anne's shoes. If only, for a moment, she could have put herself in her circumstance. If only she could have stepped into Anne's heart to understand her sorrow and the intricacies of her situation. Rather than using the Proclamation on the Family as a standard, it was used as a battering ram. When that happens, the Lord must weep.

We Are All Sisters

Years ago, I heard Sister Chieko Okazaki lovingly remind women that Relief Society—of all places—should be a society of supportive sisters where you don't have to watch what you say or worry about being labeled or judged.

Indeed, it's difficult to stand up and proclaim, "I am a mother!" when other mothers are passing judgment on your every move. I am absolutely convinced that no mother has it easy. Most mothers don't make decisions hastily, without thinking about the impact of those choices. We each do things our own way, with individualized care and attention from the Lord.

After I became a mother and realized just how hard my new career was going to be, I remember noticing other mothers in a way I hadn't before. It surprised me how interested I became in the way each sister I met mothered, her "tricks of the trade," how she coped, and the challenges she faced.

At church, I watched the mothers with six, seven, eight children . . . so beautifully coiffed and so perfectly lined up in the pew. *How in the world do they do it?* I thought. I had new appreciation and compassion for the single mother who had little or no support; the mother of three teenagers whose husband was on his second lengthy military tour overseas; the mother who deftly juggled work and family life; the mother who gave up an exciting career advancement to labor full time at home. There seemed to be as many different ways to mother as there were shoes in my friend Phyllis's expansive closet.

As I began to pay more careful attention to all of the mothers around me and reflected on my own decision to leave my career behind—to trade in sleek stilettos for a pair of sturdy running shoes—I realized that I wasn't the only woman with a story. There are *a lot* of shoes in the closet!

Each of us has a story; we each wear the shoes that best fit our circumstances and personalities. We may have one child or ten children, we may be married or divorced, we may be school-teachers or law students, PTA volunteers or community board members. Every story is different, but each includes a common thread: We are all mothers. We love our children. We love the Lord, and we want our children to love Him, too. We are sisters!

Elder Bruce C. Hafen said: "Can we love and support each other without judging each other harshly? So many of us are trying our hardest to live the commandments, often against great odds in our personal lives and unique family situations. Heaven knows, the world isn't giving us much support in these relationships. Let us support one another, even when—especially when—we differ on matters of personal choice and circumstance. Those are usually differences of preference, not principle" ("Women and the Moral Center of Gravity," in *Ye Shall Bear Record of Me*, 300).

In every woman's story there are unknowns—struggles only she knows about, fears she's tried to overcome but still harbors, disappointments and sorrows she bears. The last thing any of us wants—or needs—is to be judged by others who don't know our stories, in part or at all.

I remember a moment in homemaking meeting a few years ago when several women were chatting about the topic of motherhood. Somehow a conversation about the "appropriate" reasons to hire a baby-sitter came up. I'll never forget one sister whose comment was directed at another but which stung my heart, too. She said: "I know a woman who hires a baby-sitter every week just to get her nails done! Can you *believe* that?" I could, actually; but I also couldn't help but think that there was probably another mother in that room somewhere who also

hired a baby-sitter to give herself a short break during the week—
to do something good for herself—who might now think twice
about attending homemaking meeting next month.

My friend Whitney remembers being newly married and living and working in Manhattan. She was standing at the train station with a few women after a homemaking meeting, telling
them about a movie she had gone to see. She was so excited
about it and wanted to share her thoughts on the theme and
plot. One of her peers, who had two young children, snidely
remarked, "You clearly have too much free time. You need to
start having kids."

In each of these stories, a woman who was trying her best,
who had likely come to a church activity to feel the peace of the
gospel and associate with her sisters, was instead hurt by the
biting sting of criticism.

Elder Hafen has also observed: "If LDS women criticize each
other rather than connect with and support each other, the
adversary wins the day by driving wedges into natural, womanly
relationships of strength. Because women can give so much
never-failing charity to each other in relationships, one curse of
the modern world has been to isolate and alienate women—
including LDS women—from one another by making them
more competitive" ("Women and the Moral Center of Gravity,"
300).

"Womanly Relationships of Strength"

Instead of competing with each other, we ought to be building relationships with each other. Some of the finest examples of "womanly relationships of strength" come from the scriptures. Consider Ruth and Naomi. Naomi's family had come to Moab to escape the famine in Bethlehem. Her sons had married Moabite women—Ruth and Orpah. Then, tragedy struck. Naomi lost her husband and these two sons. She had no grandchildren. The famine being over in Bethlehem, she decided to return to her homeland, the place of her faith. Her daughters-in-law, whom she loved and who loved her in return, offered to come with her so she would not be alone.

Naomi placed the interests of these sweet daughters above her own loneliness and encouraged them to stay with their people, where they would be free to live as they might choose. Orpah did remain with the Moabites, but Ruth would not leave her mother-in-law's side. She traveled with Naomi to Bethlehem, where she labored in the fields and helped to provide for Naomi. It's apparent through the scriptures that the two had a powerful, sisterly bond. "Intreat me not to leave thee," Ruth told Naomi. "For whither thou goest, I will go; and where thou lodgest, I will lodge: thy people shall be my people, and thy God my God" (Ruth 1:16). Instead of being motivated by self-interest, these women were motivated by each other's interests.

In time, a man named Boaz heard of Ruth's kind and generous heart. The two married. Through their union, Obed was born. Obed became the father of Jesse, who became the father of David, through whom all the kings, *including the King of kings,* came.

Then there were Elisabeth and Mary, who entered motherhood at two completely different stages in life but shared a wonderful spiritual connection. When Mary learned from the angel Gabriel that she would bear the Son of God, she "went into the hill country with haste," where she met her cousin Elisabeth (Luke 1:39). The babe within Elisabeth's womb leapt as Mary entered, and Elisabeth greeted Mary "with a loud voice, and said, Blessed art thou among women, and blessed is the fruit of thy womb" (Luke 1:42). Neither woman tried to "one-up" the other. They each reveled in the other's happiness, and the two expectant mothers resided together for three months. Can you imagine their conversations? Can you imagine what they must have talked about, what feelings they may have shared about each bringing a child into the world, especially when the babies to be born each had a miraculous conception? Can you imagine the comfort, the support, and the love these women must have felt in each other's company?

Another story of two other sisters in the Bible has provided many valuable lessons for Latter-day Saint women. We all know the story of Mary and Martha and the Lord's gentle reminder to Martha to choose "that good part" (Luke 10:42). In her commentary on this New Testament account, Sister Bonnie Parkin has compared the "good part" to charity, the pure love of Christ. She says: "Do we judge one another? Do we criticize each other for individual choices, thinking we know better, when in fact we rarely understand another's unique circumstance or individual inspiration? Have we ever said, 'She works outside the home.' Or, 'Her son didn't serve a mission.' Or, 'She's too old for a calling.' Or, 'She can't—she's single.' *Such judgments, and so many others like them, rob us of the good part, that pure love of Christ"* ("Choosing Charity: That Good Part," 105; emphasis added).

Choosing the Good Part

While criticism and judgments tear us apart, charity brings us together—uniting us as sisters and women of faith.

I'll never forget a period of time when I lived in New York City. I felt spiritually drained during this time. Sometimes it was all I could do to throw on a dress and drag myself to church. But I did it. And I did it every Sunday, even though there were times when it was really hard.

Each week, the minute I walked in the door, I was quickly reminded that I was *still* single with no family, no children. I would sit alone . . . in the very back corner, in the very last pew, keeping to myself, quietly moving from meeting to meeting, praying that my soul would be uplifted just enough to carry me through another week.

I remember one Sunday leaving church, walking home through Central Park. I hadn't been home longer than ten minutes when there came a knock at the door. I opened it a crack— just wide enough to see a huge basket of vine-ripened tomatoes staring me in the face.

"You didn't quite look like yourself today," a beautiful sister said. "I just want you to know that I love you. And I am so glad you are in our ward."

Tears rolled down my face. I could not express at that moment what that act of kindness meant to me. This woman, busy with her children and her own demanding job, could have easily felt justified in labeling me "unfriendly" or "stuck-up." She could have said, "Who does she think she is?" or "Too good to talk to the rest of us?"

But she did not. She did not gossip. She did not judge. What she *did* was show me that someone cared, someone thought of me as her sister in the gospel.

What a difference a small act of charity can make in another woman's life! Charity has the power to pull us together, to make the labels we place on ourselves—and that others stick there for us—obsolete. And without the labels, we are known only as daughters of God, sisters in his great work.

Sheri Dew has said: "How often do we describe a sister with words like these: She's a convert. She's been inactive. She's a Utah Mormon. She's single. She's a stay-at-home mom.

"When we label one another, we make judgments that divide us from each other and inevitably alienate us from the Lord. The Nephites learned this lesson the hard way. After the Savior appeared on this continent, those converted to the gospel lived in harmony for two hundred years. Because they loved God, they also loved each other. And though previously there had been Nephites and Lamanites and Ishmaelites, there were now no '-ites,' as the scriptures tell us (4 Nephi 1:17). They were one. The result? There was not 'a happier people among all the people who had been created by the hand of God' (4 Nephi 1:16). It wasn't until they again divided into classes that Satan began to win many hearts. The Nephites never recovered spiritually" ("Shall We Not Go Forward in So Great a Cause," in *Arise and Shine Forth*, 27–28).

Think of the power the sisters of the Church would possess—in their homes, in their communities, in the world—if we stopped dividing each other into classes and categories!

More than twenty-five years ago, President Spencer W. Kimball prophesied that "Much of the major growth that is coming to the Church in the last days . . . will happen to the degree that the women of the Church reflect righteousness and articulateness in their lives and to the degree that they are seen as distinct and different—in happy ways—from the women of the world" (*My Beloved Sisters*, 44).

We have power, sisters! We can choose to be charitable. We can choose to walk a mile in another sister's shoes, to see things from a different perspective, to hold our tongues, and open our hearts. When we do, the Lord will notice. *I know he will.* He will bless our lives and he will bless the Church as a whole.

May we each rise to the challenge.

chapter seven

WE ARE ALL MOTHERS

We can all rejoice in the sacred calling of motherhood. To give birth is only one part of this sacred mission. . . . But to help another gain eternal life is a privilege that is neither denied to nor delayed for any worthy woman.

—Ardeth Kapp, *My Neighbor, My Sister, My Friend,* 136

For years, my favorite five minutes on network television were in a segment called "Everybody Has a Story." Every week, a wonderfully talented CBS News correspondent named Steve Hartman used a highly sophisticated piece of newsgathering equipment: a dart. He asked a person on the street to throw a dart at a map to decide where he'd go in search of a story. Once there, he would pick a name out of the phone book and inter-view that person . . . no matter who they were or what they had to say. Steve used to joke that he found stories in places only a dart would ever think to go!

People hung up on him all the time. And if they did agree to the interview, they almost always said, "Oh, *I* don't have a story . . ."

Susie Izatt was one of those people.

"Sometimes I think I'm boring and sometimes I think I'm a nobody," she told Steve when he showed up, camera rolling, at her home in Westmoreland County, Pennsylvania. But Susie is anything but a nobody; and her story is one of the great reminders in this world that the *best* stories are found in the simplest places and based on the simplest theme: love.

Susie and her husband, Jim, are the parents of three vibrant—and demanding—sons: Josh, Dennis, and Joey.

The fact that Susie and Jim now *have* three children is some-what of a miracle.

On Susie's twenty-fifth birthday, she had a hysterectomy, wiping out her dreams of having a baby. But Susie is a woman of faith. She believed that God must have a plan for her—even if that plan didn't involve actually *bearing* children.

Five years later, the couple adopted Josh. They desperately wanted to adopt more children, but the waiting list was discouragingly long—so many other couples were anxiously waiting for their chance to adopt, too.

So Susie and Jim did the next best thing: they decided to become foster parents. Soon, Dennis and Joey were placed in the Izatts' home.

By the time they got there, Dennis and Joey had been through a lot in their young lives. When Susie first met the boys she said they displayed "almost animal-like behavior. They would claw at people. They weren't properly toilet trained. And they didn't know how to use silverware."

By the time Steve Hartman visited the Izatt home for his story, the boys had made remarkable progress. They could use silverware *and* chopsticks. They showed Steve scrapbooks full of pictures from outings and their many other adventures. They talked about climbing trees, playing ball, and doing all the things little boys are supposed to do in their childhood years.

All of this because one woman believed God had a plan for her and was willing to change her course—and her mind-set— so she could become part of these little boys' lives.

As Steve interviewed the family, it was obvious that Joey and Dennis belonged with the Izatts; and the Izatts belonged with them.

Steve finished his interview by asking the two boys, "What is the *one* thing you want most?"

Joey's wish was simple: "Can I be adopted?"

The answer, of course, was yes. Shortly after the interview, a judge signed the papers and made Joey and Dennis members of the Izatt family. Says Susie, "The love that we have in our family is more than I'd ever want. . . . It's so fulfilling. It is so good."

In the last line of the story, Steve (with a wink and a smile) said this: "So, that's the story of the boring woman from Pennsylvania, who thinks she's a nobody, with absolutely nothing interesting going on in her life. . . . Steve Hartman, CBS News" (*CBS Evening News,* December 18, 1999).

Sometimes—many times—the path God has placed before us is not the path we would have chosen for ourselves. I am certainly following a plan different from the one I had in mind twenty years ago. But, like Susie, what I have now is more fulfilling than I ever imagined.

Every woman has the opportunity to feel this same sense of fulfillment—this blessed measure of happiness—that Susie Izatt speaks of. How do we achieve it? I believe we do it by turning ourselves over to the Lord and by then tapping into the part of ourselves that innately and instinctively knows how to nurture and love others—the part that knows how to mother.

Sixteen years ago, Sister Ardeth G. Kapp told a story in one of her books that has stayed with me ever since. Sister Kapp, who did not bear any children of her own but certainly mothered thousands as she led the Young Women of the Church, wrote: "I will forever remember the day a child new to our neighborhood knocked on our door and asked if our children could come out to play. I explained to him, as to others young and old, for the thousandth time, that we didn't have any children. This little boy squinted his eyes in a quizzical look and asked the question I had not dared put into words, 'If you are not a mother, then what are you?'" (*My Neighbor, My Sister, My Friend*, 123).

What a question! Sister Kapp went on to describe the depth of emotion and the struggle she faced as a woman of faith who had not been blessed with children of her own. She acknowledged that it took time—years, really—to be at peace with her circumstance, to know what God knows. And that knowledge is this: *every* woman can find happiness and fulfillment in mothering. "You need not possess children to love them. Loving is not synonymous with possessing, and possessing is not necessarily loving. The world is filled with people to be loved, guided, taught, lifted, and inspired" (*My Neighbor, My Sister, My Friend*, 126).

Sisters, I believe this. I have witnessed it over and over again—In my own life, in my girlfriends' lives, and in the lives of the many women I have had the honor of meeting around the world. We are all mothers. Every day we take part in amazing stories about "ordinary" women who perform the extraordinary

work of motherhood. Every day is the perfect day to find someone who can be "loved, guided, taught, lifted, and inspired."

Mothering around the World

One of the most touching stories I covered during my years
at KSL in Salt Lake City was the story of eleven-year-old Charlie
Hays.

I first met Charlie and his mother, Susan, in Malibu,
California, around Mother's Day.

Charlie hadn't come to California for a vacation. Charlie had
come to California to die. Four years earlier, this handsome,
blond-haired little boy had been diagnosed with cancer of the
thyroid. For years, he outlived the doctors' expectations; but then
the cancer took over his body. Tumors clogged his lungs and
lined his bones.

As it became more and more apparent that Charlie would
not be able to last much longer, he expressed his final wish.
Charlie and his family had recently been to the California coast
on vacation. Charlie loved it there. He loved to see the dolphins
swim and feel the sea breeze on his face. As they were leaving to
return home, Charlie said to his mom, "This is the most beautiful place I've ever seen. This is where I want to die."

As you can imagine, that was an emotionally overwhelming

request for his mother—and one that seemed financially out of reach for their family.

So Susan placed an ad in a Malibu newspaper, offering to clean house, baby-sit children, or trade her home in Park City, Utah, for a room with a view of the surf.

The newspaper editor noticed the ad at the bottom of the classifieds and turned it into a front-page spread.

Susan's phone began to ring off the hook.

And then one very generous stranger left her family speechless.

This kind stranger, a woman who declined being interviewed for my story because she wanted to remain anonymous, offered up her beautiful, three-bedroom beach house, free, for as long as Charlie needed it.

She stocked the house with groceries, installed handrails to make it easier for Charlie to get up and down the stairs, provided medical supplies, including an oxygen tank, and enlisted the service of a local physician, on-call for Charlie around the clock.

And so it was that Charlie and his mother ended up in Malibu on Mother's Day. It was the last Mother's Day Charlie's mother would spend with her son. Charlie died soon after. He was twelve years old.

As I met with this family, I could feel their turmoil. I remembered the overwhelming feelings of pain and loss I had experienced years ago as I watched my own brother slip away. But I also felt a measure of peace: peace coming in with the calming lull of the ocean's tide; peace in a boy's heart because his mother would be by his side as he slipped to the other side; and peace in a mother's heart because another woman had reached out—in love—to help fulfill a final wish.

It was that stranger's gift—her ability to give selflessly and humbly—that has stayed with me for so long. For, just as Charlie needed his mother's love during this difficult time, Charlie's *mother* needed to be lifted by the mother-like love this kind woman willingly offered her.

Thousands of miles from the California coast, I met another amazing woman who possessed many of the same humble qualities as Charlie's anonymous benefactor.

I traveled to Shantou, China, to write and produce a documentary about a group of volunteer medical workers—doctors and nurses—who had come to China, at their own expense, to operate on children with terrible, disfiguring facial deformities.

What I saw when I first arrived at the dirty, run-down hospital in Shantou took my breath away. Hundreds upon hundreds of parents and little children were huddled together, waiting in lines, each parent hoping that their child would be chosen to receive this life-changing surgery.

One of those in line was a sixty-five-year-old grandmother,

her belongings stuffed in a black plastic bag, a little baby strapped around her chest with a big white cloth, and a huge smile on her face.

This woman was very religious. Every morning, as was her custom, she would walk to the Buddhist temple to pray.

One morning, as she was walking up the steps of the temple, she literally stumbled upon a newborn baby. This tiny babe had been left to die, cloth and paper stuffed in her mouth, because of her disfiguring cleft lip and palate.

The woman had a child and a grandchild of her own and already lived a very humble life. But her mother-heart would not let her turn away. She scooped up that little baby and vowed at that moment she would take care of her. She knew this little child needed to be "loved, guided, taught, lifted, and inspired."

She had heard about the American doctors and so began her journey to find them, carrying her fragile load for three days by train and on foot—a distance of almost 300 miles.

The doctors took her baby and, within a few days, the child—nicknamed the Buddha baby—was reborn. No more cleft lip and palate. She could now eat and smile freely and live a normal life.

When my cameraman and I went back to China a year later, we tracked down the little Buddha baby. She was a completely different child—happy, healthy, well-adjusted. All because a woman, who probably thought her mothering days were over, knew that we are all mothers—always. She gave of herself in order to give another human being the one thing we all need most: love.

On another reporting assignment, in April 1999, I met a whole town full of people who, like the grandmother in China, were led by the Spirit—even if they didn't know that's what it was—to love, guide, teach, lift, and inspire an entire town.

I had been sent to Macedonia, to cover the plight of thousands of Albanian refugees who had been forced, at gunpoint, from their homes and from their homeland by Serbian dictator Slobodan Milosevic. They were the victims of a religious war—a late-twentieth-century holocaust that killed tens of thousands of innocent people in central Europe.

These refugees had done nothing wrong. They were good, hard-working, middle-class people—teachers, accountants, shop owners. But because they were of a certain religion, they were persecuted, driven from their homes, raped, tortured, and killed.

Thousands upon thousands of families were dumped in a stark, muddy, rank refugee camp at the Kosovo–Macedonia border by Serbian trains that ran through the area twenty-four hours a day, seven days a week. This camp was filled mostly with women and children, left alone because their husbands and fathers had been killed.

One day during our assignment, my producer, camera crew, and I left the camp to travel to a picturesque hamlet high in the mountains of Macedonia. The town was called Molina, and it was just a few hundred feet from the Kosovo border. It took us almost nine hours to drive there, sometimes in treacherous conditions.

Well, we finally made it. And was it ever worth the trip!

Geographically, this was one of the most beautifully pristine places I had ever seen, literally perched on top of a mountain. And the people of Molina were just as beautiful, some of the kindest and most humble I have ever met. They truly allowed the Lord to use them for good.

This tiny town of 600 had grown to almost *1,600* overnight.

It had happened in the wee hours of the morning. Close to one thousand refugees, scurrying to escape across the border, had been walking for almost twenty-four hours when they arrived in Molina in the middle of a cold, rainy night. Exhausted, hungry, fumbling through the darkness, they had no idea of the generosity that awaited them.

As these refugees literally stumbled into this little village, slowly—one by one—the lamps inside Molina's small, modest homes flickered to life. The townspeople had awakened to welcome their bewildered and unexpected guests.

These mostly poor farmers offered the refugees everything

they had. The women fired up their ovens and baked fresh bread until the sun rose. They turned over their homes, their beds, their extra clothing, everything they had, to strangers.

One woman told me: "We can hardly afford to provide for our own families . . . but they knocked on our doors and we must help them."

I remember one extended family of thirteen who welcomed another *fifty-one* people into their modest little home. "They were almost dying from walking so long," the mother told our cameras. "We will share our very last piece of bread with them."

That morning, even the children joined in the greeting. The villagers donned their best outfits and danced to the sound of one violin. And in one moment, hundreds of people felt music in their hearts and captured a little piece of home.

Mothers Look toward the Light

Three years later, I found myself on another story in another city. This time I was in my own backyard: New York City. The setting was much different from the little village outside Kosovo, but the hope I saw in the children's eyes was the same.

It was about six months after the horrific events of September 11, and I was visiting an elementary school next to Ground Zero in Lower Manhattan.

This school stood, literally, in the shadow of the World Trade

Center. Many children in the schoolyard that day had watched the planes slam into those buildings. These little ones escaped with their lives as the first tower came crashing down. With their teachers, hand–in-hand, they ran almost two miles to safety.

I was doing a documentary for PBS, and we went to this school because, after six months, the students were just returning to their classrooms and First Lady Laura Bush was there to talk to them and to comfort them.

The kids opened up about a lot of things: how difficult it was to move past what happened. How they still had nightmares. Why some of their friends' parents didn't make it out of the towers that Tuesday morning.

The principal talked about how brave and resilient her students were . . . and what it was like to be back in a place full of so many awful memories. I asked her what the biggest change in school was since the children had come back to class.

Without hesitation she said simply: "It's the light."

This little school had literally been in the shadow of those towers. And now that the buildings were gone, every room was filled with glowing light.

A powerful metaphor—and a vivid, stinging reminder—of what was literally missing next door.

That day, one of the teachers said something that had a real impact on me. She said, "When my kids are sad or discouraged or enduring a difficult day, I tell them: 'Look up. Look up toward the light . . . and think of one thing you have to be grateful for.'"

"Look up toward the light." Even in the darkest hours, there is light, and there is hope.

It is this light and hope that women so ably distribute to all who enter their lives. It is this light and hope that enables all women to mother—to recognize that "the world is filled with people to be loved, guided, taught, lifted, and inspired."

Our ability to mother our own children—to mother all children, really—is an innate gift bestowed upon us by a gracious Father in Heaven who loves us and knows what we can become.

Not "Just a Mother"

I have experienced the loving "mothering" of so many wonderful women in my life. My own mother, my mother-in-law, my grandmothers, my dear sister, my friends—even Phyllis Diller, with her closet full of shoes and her heart full of love—have mothered me through the years. Their love has been imprinted on my heart—a reminder of my own calling as a mother and woman of faith.

Sister Sheri Dew says, "Every time we build the faith or reinforce the nobility of a young woman or man, every time we love or lead anyone even one small step along the path, we are true to our endowment and calling as mothers and in the process we build the kingdom of God. No woman who understands the gospel would ever think that any other work is more important or would ever say, 'I am *just* a mother,' for *mothers heal the souls of men*" ("Are We Not All Mothers?" 97).

Mothers do heal the souls of men! I know this; and because I know it, I will never feel like I am *just* a mother.

Not too long ago, Mark and I were in Florida with newborn Ella and Mark's children, visiting Mark's mom. One morning after breakfast, we were all walking through the lobby of the hotel. I had our children in tow and probably looked a little frazzled, dressed in my "mommy clothes," hair pulled back, no makeup on. Suddenly, from across the room, I heard someone say, "Jane, Jane—is that you?"

I turned around to see a rather famous old friend, someone I had profiled and interviewed years before on *The Early Show*. He looked just the same: immaculately dressed and pressed. *I* looked quite different, with a baby in arms, diaper bag over my shoulder, three older kids corralled at my side, and clad in my fabulous "new-mom" wardrobe.

After a round of introductions, this fellow looked at me and said:

"So . . . what are you up to these days—" he paused and looked down at my kids, "just a mom?"

In a split second I had to decide. . . . What was I going to say?

What came out of my mouth surprised me at first . . . but also made me very happy. *Just a mom?* I thought.

"No!" I proclaimed, with a smile. "No . . . I am a mother!"

He seemed puzzled.

And then he grinned.

He got my message.

Sisters, we are all mothers! There are no *justs* involved. And as mothers, as women of God, we each have a story to tell, to share with our children and their children and all the children whose lives we touch.

This is my story—at least the beginning of it.

May you share yours—along with your love, your faith, and your courage—with everyone in your life.

Works Cited

Arise and Shine Forth: Talks from the 2000 Women's Conference Sponsored by Brigham Young University and the Relief Society. Salt Lake City: Bookcraft, 2001.

Beauty of Motherhood, The: Selected Writings about the Joys of Being a Mother. Compiled by Bette Bishop. Kansas City, Mo.: Hallmark, 1967.

Bednar, David A. "The Tender Mercies of the Lord," *Ensign,* May 2005.

Bush, Barbara. *Barbara Bush: A Memoir.* New York: St. Martin's Press, 1995.

Children's Songbook. Salt Lake City: The Church of Jesus Christ of Latter-day Saints, 1989.

Clark, J. Reuben Jr. "The Message of the First Presidency to the Church," *Improvement Era,* November 1942.

Crittenden, Ann. *The Price of Motherhood: Why the Most Important Job in the World Is Still the Least Valued.* New York: Henry Holt and Company, 2001.

Dew, Sheri. "Are We Not All Mothers?" *Ensign*, November 2001.

Faust, James, E. "A Messsage to My Granddaughters," *Ensign*, September 1986.

Hinckley, Gordon B. "In the Arms of His Love," *Ensign*, November 2006.

———. "Life's Obligations," *Ensign*, February 1999.

———. *Teachings of Gordon B. Hinckley*. Salt Lake City: Deseret Book, 1997.

Holland, Jeffrey R. "Because She Is a Mother," *Ensign*, May 1997.

Holland, Jeffrey R., and Patricia T. *On Earth As It Is in Heaven*. Salt Lake City: Deseret Book, 1989.

Kapp, Ardeth G. *My Neighbor, My Sister, My Friend*. Salt Lake City, Utah: Deseret Book, 1990.

Kimball, Spencer W. *My Beloved Sisters*. Salt Lake City, Utah: Bookcraft, 1979.

———. "The Role of Righteous Women," *Ensign*, November 1979.

Lee, Harold B. *Teachings of Harold B. Lee*. Edited by Clyde J. Williams. Salt Lake City: Bookcraft, 1996.

Lewis, C. S. *Mere Christianity: A Revised and Amplified Edition*. San Francisco: HarperSanFrancisco, 2001.

Maxwell, Neal A. *If Thou Endure It Well*. Salt Lake City: Bookcraft, 1996.

———. *On Becoming a Disciple Scholar*. Edited by Henry B. Eyring. Salt Lake City: Bookcraft, 1995.

———. "The Women of God," *Ensign*, May 1978.

McKay, David O. *Gospel Ideals: Selections from the Discourses of David O. McKay*. Salt Lake City: *Improvement Era*, 1953.

Northrup, Christiane. *Mother-Daughter Wisdom: Creating a Legacy of Physical and Emotional Health*. New York: Bantam Dell, 2005.

Old Testament Gospel Doctrine Teacher's Manual. Salt Lake City: The Church of Jesus Christ of Latter-day Saints, 1996.

Parkin, Bonnie. "Choosing Charity: That Good Part," *Ensign*, November 2003.

Peace: Essays of Hope and Encouragement. Salt Lake City: Deseret Book, 1998.

Quindlen, Anna. *Loud and Clear*. New York: Random House, 2004.

Roberts, Cokie. *We Are Our Mothers' Daughters*. New York: Harper Collins, 2000.

Smith, Joseph F. *Gospel Doctrine: Selections from the Sermons and Writings of Joseph F. Smith*. Salt Lake City: Deseret Book, 1939.

———. *Teachings of Presidents of the Church: Joseph F. Smith*. Salt Lake City: The Church of Jesus Christ of Latter-day Saints, 1998.

Tanner, Susan W. "Strengthening Future Mothers," *Ensign*, June 2005.

Winfrey, Oprah. "What I Know for Sure," *O, The Oprah Magazine*, May 2003.

Woman. Salt Lake City: Deseret Book Company, 1979.

Ye Shall Bear Record of Me: Talks from the 2001 BYU Women's Conference. Salt Lake City: Bookcraft, 2002.

INDEX

Adoption, 113–15
Airport, 77–80
Albanian refugees, 121–23
Anker, Inger Elizabeth, 57
Attic, 91–92
Avis, 77–80

Babies, holding, 14–17
Babysitters, reasons for hiring,
    104–5
Bednar, David A., on Lord's
    timing, 36
Bedroom, 91–92
Big picture, 80–81, 87
Blessing, from Neal A. Maxwell,
    28–29
Bonaparte, Napoleon, on mothers,
    53
Bonding, 14–17
Breaks, taking time for, 84–88
Buddha baby, 119–21

Bush, Barbara, on importance of
    homes, xi

California, 117–19
Cancer, 62–64, 117–19
Cards, greeting, 62
Career: choosing motherhood
    over, 1–5; early, of Jane
    Clayson Johnson, 21–28; Jane
    Clayson Johnson leaves,
    36–39; motherhood as,
    42–44
Caregiving, 60–61
Carsickness, 81–83
Charity, 108–11
Charlston, South Carolina, 77–80
Children: teaching importance of
    family to, 56–58; teaching,
    60–65; grow up quickly, 88;
    step, 89–92; Rebekah prays
    for, 93–95; adopted, 113–15

China, grandmother adopts baby in, 119–21

Church of Jesus Christ of Latter-day Saints, The: reconciling career with, 30–31, 33–34; criticism among members of, 104–5; Spencer W. Kimball on women's righteousness and growth of, 110–11

Clark, J. Reuben Jr., on divinity and motherhood, 6

Clayson, Beulah, 57

Clayson, David, 62–64

Clayson Johnson, Jane: chooses motherhood over career, 1–5; education and early career of, 21–28; anchors for *The Early Show,* 28–34; mother brings coat to, 53–56; mother of, as example of service, 61–64; receives service during difficult time, 71–74; flies to wrong Charleston, 77–80

Cleft palate, 119–21

Clothing, modesty in choosing, 65–70

Coat, Jane's, brought to her, 53–56

Coffee, 30–31

Competition, 105

Conference call, 30–31

Control, 77–81

Criticism, 104–5, 108–11

Crittenden, Ann: on value of motherhood, 43; on skillful caregiving, 60–61

Dart, 112–15

Daughters of God, Spencer W. Kimball on, 64

Dew, Sheri: on importance of mothers, 8–9; on motherhood as ennobling endowment, 50; on labeling others, 110; on fulfilling callings as mothers, 125–26

Diller, Phyllis, 96–100

Divinity, motherhood and, 5–7

Dole, Bob, 53–56

Early Show, The, 28–34

eBay, 50–51

Elisabeth, Mary's cousin, 107

Endurance, 74–76

Equality, 93

Eternal perspective, 80–81, 87

Faith, 112–15

Family: teaching children importance of, 56–58; mission statement for, 64–65

"Family, The: A Proclamation to the World," 100–102

France, 53

Friendship, 81–84

Genealogy, 56–58

Generosity, toward refugees, 121–23

God: Neal A. Maxwell on submission to will of, 18, 39; submitting to will of, 19–21, 115–17; following timelines of, 21–28, 36; Jeffrey R. Holland on submission to will of, 38; C. S. Lewis on being shaped by, 52; Spencer W. Kimball on daughters of, 64;

motherhood as means to
identify with, 89
Gratitude, for light, 123–25
Gray, Meredith, on motherhood, 1
Gumble, Bryant, 28

Hafen, Bruce C.: on devaluing
motherhood, 45–46; on
influence of mothers, 59; on
supporting each other
without judgment, 104; on
criticizing each other, 105
Hanks, Marion D., 83–84
Hartman, Steve, 112–15
Hays, Charlie, 117–19
Hinckley, Gordon B.: on divinity
and motherhood, 6; on Jesus
Christ as friend in
motherhood, 83–84; on
taking breaks, 86
Holland, Jeffrey R.: on difficulty in
mothering, xi; on mothering
as God's work, 16–17; on
Jesus Christ's submission to
God's will, 20–21; on
submission to God's will, 38;
on relying on Jesus Christ, 71
Holland, Patricia, on Satan's
attack on women, 47–48
Homes, Barbara Bush on, xi
Honor: for mothers, 40–41; for
family, 56–58
Hope, Bob, 96–97
House, analogy of, 52

Identity, loss of, as myth, 88–92
"If You're Happy," 95
Illness, supporting husband and
children through, 100–102

Industrial revolution, 43–44
Izatt, Susie, 112–15

Jesus Christ: mothers as co-
partners with, 14–17;
submission to God's will of,
20–21; Jeffrey R. Holland on
relying on, 71; as friend in
motherhood, 83–84
Johnson, Adriana, 57
Johnson, Mark, influence of
mother on, 40–41
Johnson, Whitney, 64–65
Johnson, William, 71–74
Judging others, 100–105, 108–11

Kapp, Ardeth G.: on rejoicing in
motherhood, 112; on love
and mothering, 115–16
Kimball, Spencer W.: on daughters
of God, 64; on righteous
women, 69; on women's
righteousness and growth of
Church, 110–11
Kindness: Jane Clayson Johnson
receives, 109; for Charlie and
Susan Hays, 117–19; for
refugees, 121–23

Labels, 109–11
Lee, Harold B., on influence of
mothers, 59
Lewis, C. S., on being shaped by
God, 52
Light, importance of, 123–25
Los Angeles, 25–28
Love: sharing, 115–17; for Charlie
and Susan Hays, 117–19; for
Buddha baby, 119–21; for
refugees, 121–23
Lynch, Jessica, 77–80

Macedonia, 121–23

Marriage, 36

Martha, 107–8

Mary, 107

Maxwell, Neal A.: on influence of mothers, 5; on submission to God's will, 18, 39; blessing from, 28–29

McConkie, Bruce R., on mothers receiving revelation, 94–95

McKay, David O., on influence of mothers, 14

Measurables, 47–48

Men, equality of women and, 93

Milosevic, Slobodan, 121

Mission statement, of family, 64–65

Modesty, 65–70

Monson, Thomas S., on Satan's attack on motherhood, 47

Moses, 86–87

Mother's Day, 117–19

Motherhood: difficulty and importance of, xii–xiii; choosing, over career, 1–5; as divine calling, 5–7; changing attitudes about, 7–13; influence of, 13–14, 58–60; co-partnering with Jesus Christ in, 14–17; Jane Clayson Johnson leaves career for, 36–39; honoring, 40–41; as career, 42–44; valuing, 44–49; as season of life, 50–52; thoughtfulness and, 53–56; teaching children and, 60–65; being unafraid and invincible in, 65–70; as test of endurance, 74–76;

preparation for, 76–77; control as myth of, 77–81; not needing help as myth of, 81–84; doing it all as myth of, 84–88; loss of identity as myth of, 88–92; receiving revelations on, 92–95; supporting women in, 100–105; having charity in, 108–11; finding happiness and fulfillment in, 115–17; expressing pride in, 126–27

Mother Teresa, 18–19

Myth: control in motherhood as, 77–81; not needing help as, 81–84; doing it all as, 84–88; loss of identity as, 88–92

Naomi, 106–7

New York City, 28–34

Nilson, Ellen, 57

Northrup, Christiane, on influence of mothers, 58–59

Occupation, 11

Okazaki, Chieko, 102

Palace, 52

Parkin, Bonnie, on charity and criticizing, 108

Pencil, analogy of, 18–19

Photo shoot, 68–69

Plans, Jane's, for life, 21–28

Pratt, Malona, 57

Prayer, for Rebekah's children, 93–95

Premature baby, 71–74

Pride, 126–27

Prom dress, 66–67

Quindlen, Anna: on importance of mothering, xii; on success, 35; on influence of mothers, 40; on friendship between mothers, 83

Rat race, 35
Rebekah, 93–95
Refugees, 121–23
Relief Society, as support system, 102
Religion, reconciling career with, 30–34
Revelations, 92–95
Roberts, Cokie, on value of motherhood, 43–44
Ruth, 106–7

Sacrifices, 89, 91–92
Satan, attack on motherhood of, 46–47, 88–92
School, in shadow of World Trade Center, 123–25
Seasons of a woman's life, 50–52
Self-worth, xiii
September 11, 2001, terrorist attacks, 34–35, 123–25
Service, 62–64, 71–74, 109
Shoes: Phyllis Diller and, 96–100; walking in other women's, 100–105
Shriver, Maria, on empowering mothers, 7
Simpson, O. J., 26–27
Smith, Emma, submission to God's will of, 19–20
Smith, Joseph F.: on being a successful parent, 49; on Eliza R.

Snow, 65; on leading women, 96
Snow, Eliza R., Joseph F. Smith on, 65
Soup, homemade chicken noodle, 85–86
Stepchildren, 89–92
Stratford, Gladys, 57
Strength, relationships of, 106–8
Struggles, 44–45
Submission: Neal A. Maxwell on, 18, 39; to God's will, 19–21, 115–17; Jeffrey R. Holland on, 38
Success: definition of, 11; Anna Quindlen on, 35; measuring, 47–48; Joseph F. Smith on, 49
Supermom, 84–88
Support, importance of, 100–105

Tanner, N. Eldon, on influence of mothers, 60
Tanner, Susan W., 10
Testimonies, 60–65
Thompson, Lorenda, 57
Time-out, importance of, for self, 84–88
Timing, 21–28, 36, 115–17
Tomatoes, 109
Tomlin, Lily, 35
Trials: in motherhood, 44–45; enduring, 74–76

USA Today, 42

Wallace, William Ross, on influence of mothers, 75
Weakness, needing help is not, 81–84

Whitman, Meg, 50–51

Will of God: Neal A. Maxwell on submission to, 18, 39; submitting to, 19–21, 115–17; Jeffrey R. Holland on submission to, 38

Winfrey, Oprah, on importance of mothers, 7–8

Women: worth of, xiii; Spencer W. Kimball on righteous, 69; equality of men and, 93; Joseph F. Smith on leading, 96; supporting other, 100–105; strengthening relationships between, 106–8

Working, 100–102

World Trade Center, 34–35, 123–25